The
Ottoman Empire
and the
World Economy

SUNY Series in Middle Eastern Studies
Shahrough Akahavi, Editor

THE
OTTOMAN EMPIRE
AND THE
WORLD ECONOMY

—The Nineteenth Century—

Reşat Kasaba

State University of New York

Cover: Loading fruit in İzmir, 1863.
(*Illustrated London News*, XLII,
August 22, 1863, p. 201.)

Published by
State University of New York Press, Albany

For information, address State University of New York
Press, State University Plaza, Albany, N.Y., 12246

Library of Congress Cataloging-in-Publication Data

Kasaba, Reşat, 1954-
The Ottoman empire and the world-economy: the nineteenth century
Reşat Kasaba.
     p. cm. — (SUNY series in Middle Eastern studies)
  Bibliography: p.
  Includes index.
  ISBN 0-88706-804-9. ISBN 0-88706-805-7 (pbk.)
  1. Turkey—Economic conditions. 2. Turkey—Commerce—History—19th century. 3.
Turkey—Foreign economic relations—Europe. 4. Europe—Foreign economic relations—
Turkey. 5. Turkey—History—19th century. 6. Turkey—Politics and government—19
century. I. Title. II. Series.
HO492.K37 1988   88-3039
                                                                        CIP

10 9 8 7 6 5 4 3

To my father
Muzzaffer Kasaba,
and to the memory of
my mother,
Handan Kasaba

Contents

Tables

Acknowledgments

MANY PEOPLE contributed their guidance, friendship, and trust to this study. At times like this, one wishes to remember all of them only to realize that it is impossible to do so. Even though the following is only a partial list, it still demonstrates the breadth and depth of expertise and assistance one needs to tap in order to proceed with a project like this one.

I wish to thank Çağlar Keyder for setting the agenda; Immanuel Wallerstein, Terence K. Hopkins, and Giovanni Arrighi for providing the vision; Şevket Pamuk, and Donald Quataert for their valuable advice and constant encouragement. The National Science Foundation provided a fellowship which made most of the original research possible. The professional staffs at the Public Record Office in London, the Archeological Museum in Izmir, and the Glenn G. Bartle Library at the State University of New York at Binghamton were very helpful in locating the key documents I used in writing this book. Halil İnalcık, Huri İnan, and Martin Murray were also among the initiators; Kenneth Barr, Bill Martin, Faruk Tabak, Ravi Palat, Roger Owen, and Zafer Toprak shared their ideas with me; Necmi Ülker provided an introduction to the court records in İzmir; Zeki Ezer helped me with the transliteration of the Ottoman Turkish material; Donna DeVoist was pivotal in creating an atmosphere that was conducive to research and writing at the Fernand Braudel Center; Jere Bacharach, Daniel Chirot, Joel Migdal, and Felicia Hecker helped me make an easy transition from Binghamton to Seattle

xi

where this book took its final form; Margery Lang read the original draft and smoothed the rough edges of my prose; Nancy Acheson typed the manuscript and contributed her suggestions while doing an excellent job. Of the SUNY Press, William Eastman and Bernadine Dawes have been very cooperative in the preparation of this book. Finally, with their trust and support, Harriet Friedman, Harold Friedman, Kerime Senyücel, and Münip Senyücel helped ease some of the more difficult periods of research and writing. I am grateful to these individuals and institutions for all the help they have given me. A special note of appreciation goes to Kathie who has been an integral part of this project since its beginning. I feel fortunate that I have been privy to her intellectual breadth and that she shared the joys of this work's progress while lessening its frustrations.

Chapter two is a shorter and revised version of an article which previously appeared in *Review* X, 5/6 (supplement), Summer-Fall 1987. I thank the editors for giving me permission for using it here.

1

Introduction

THE FORMAL EXISTENCE of the Ottoman Empire on the world historical scene extends from ca. 1300 to the end of the First World War. Most Ottoman specialists have chosen to concentrate on the last phase of this broad spectrum of history in quest of discovering the reasons for its decline. In this literature, it was the norm until recently to portray the last century of the empire as years of military defeat, economic ruin, and political ineptitude culminating in catastrophe and total collapse. At the same time, it is argued that important trends toward the improvement of administrative structure, educational system, and transportation and communication networks also took root in the empire during these years. Eventually the latter trend emerged as the predominant theme of the century and proved to be the determining phenomenon in the establishment of the Turkish Republic following the formal disappearance of the Ottoman Empire.

This approach, which until recently held exclusive sway over the writing of Ottoman history, presents three crucial problems. First, although the deterioration of the overall Ottoman system and the modernization of some of its institutions were taking place simultaneously, these two processes are never analyzed together. Furthermore, some recent studies have shown that the Ottoman economy, far from being in ruins, exhibited some very impressive signs of vitality during the nineteenth century.[1] Thus, intertwined with the retrogression of the

1

empire, there was intermittent economic growth, and both of these processes were tapped by a political superstructure that was undergoing a fairly radical reorganization itself. Rather than being construed as separate fields of inquiry, the processes that relate to the decline of classical institutions, economic growth, and administrative reorganization must be analyzed together.

Second, even though it is generally accepted that the European powers were centrally involved in this dual process of decline and growth, the nature and consequences of their involvement are treated in an ambiguous way. By far the most common form of analyzing Euro-Ottoman relations in the nineteenth century has been a recourse to interstate diplomacy. This has produced volumes of meticulously catalogued treaties, memoranda, private correspondence, and the like. By itself, such documentation is of little help in clarifying the European impact on the dissolution of the Ottoman Empire. Political, cultural, and economic aspects of Euro-Ottoman relations were related to each other, and they must be assessed as such. To be able to do this, however, we must start by locating the whole array of processes that emanated from Europe in a broader theoretical and historical framework.

The third problem, in addition to being a source of confusion by itself, also accentuates the difficulties caused by the first two. From its very beginnings, the writing of Ottoman history has adopted an almost exclusive focus on state and has relied primarily on state-related sources and documentation. The bureaucratic apparatus, which the Ottomans administered for six hundred years, generated voluminous material, most of which still awaits unearthing and deciphering. Consequently, historiography has developed in a staggering manner with gaping "dark ages" resulting from lack or inaccessibility of documents and, most important, without any unifying theme. Furthermore, the nature of the sources that are used have tainted the resulting interpretations with a bias toward the Ottoman state where all the structures and transformations of the Ottoman Empire are analyzed and evaluated through the prism of the central government. It is imperative that we broaden this resource base and include extrastate documents in our analysis to have a better grasp of not only the position of the Ottoman governments within the changing circumstances of the nineteenth century but also to adequately understand *social* change in the Ottoman Empire.

Each of the three problems that I have outlined above involves the various aspects of the processes of the disintegration of the Ottoman Empire and its transformation in a manner that created the conditions for the subsequent development of the Turkish Republic. Most Ottoman scholars tend to set the two processes apart in time and place and analyze them separately. The main purpose of this book is to bring these two processes in relation to each other and to demonstrate that they were intertwined, simultaneous aspects of the broader process of the integration of the Ottoman Empire into the capitalist world economy.[2]

GENERAL THEORETICAL AND HISTORICAL CONSIDERATIONS

Classical Age

I refer to the history of the Ottoman Empire up to the sixteenth century as its "classical age." During that period the Ottoman Empire was an expanding world empire; the type of domination exercised by its rulers was patrimonial; and the empire was integrated through the operation of a redistributive-tributary network. The three concepts—world empire, patrimonialism, and redistributive-tributary mode of integration—are derived respectively from the works of Wallerstein, Weber, and Polanyi. As a world empire, the Ottoman Empire is defined as having a single social economy (i.e., division of labor) with an overarching political structure.[3] Patrimonialism describes this political structure as having a well-defined center which exercises its authority through a large administrative staff. In this configuration, ultimate ownership of economic and administrative means (and hence power) remained vested in the imperial center. The bureaucratic offshoots of this apparatus wielded power locally but only in the name of and as derived from the center.[4] Redistributive-tributary mode is used to characterize the main axis of integration of the imperial system. According to this, the fruits of land and labor flowed from the producing class of subjects to the nonproducing class of rulers for the latter's use and consumption. In the opposite direction, goods and titles to resources were redistributed within the framework of political parameters and priorities that the rulers had set for themselves.[5] Together, these three characteristics were constitutive of the Ottoman Empire as a historical unit of analysis by itself.

World Economy

In this book, the capitalist world economy refers to the historically specific system of economic relations that was centralized in northwestern Europe during the fifteenth and sixteenth centuries. In the course of the following four centuries, this system has expanded by incorporating areas that had hitherto been external to its operations. The capitalist world economy is characterized by the existence of a single division of labor; but unlike world empires, it contains multiple state structures. As its organizing principle, this division of labor embodies economic, and specifically capitalist, rationality; this means that it is geared towards endless accumulation of capital.

The relative place of geographical regions along the axial division of labor of the capitalist world economy has depended on a number of historically determined factors. These factors and the relative position of different areas have varied, but the resultant alignment has always been hierarchical, thus lending itself to a tripartite division as core, semiperiphery, and periphery. These three zones reflect the trimodal distribution of the returns that are generated by the integrated processes of production that characterize the capitalist world economy. A parallel gradient from state structures that are relatively strong to those that are relatively weak reinforces this basic structure. In this configuration, the boundaries that delineate the state structures never correspond fully to those that define the economic zones.

The growth of the capitalist world economy has been cyclical with alternating periods of economic expansion and contraction, as was initially demonstrated by Kondratieff.[6] Intertwined with these long waves has been the continuous widening and deepening of the characteristic relations of the capitalist world economy involving the integration of new areas into its division of labor.[7]

The processes that incorporate an external area into the world economy are not always identical or coterminous with those that define its status within that system. In the case of the Ottoman Empire, we will distinguish the two parts of this process as incorporation and peripheralization, respectively.

Incorporation

Incorporation refers to a twofold process: one is the establishment of links between the production processes of an external arena and the loci of production and consumption in the capitalist world economy; the other, is the integration of the political structures of this area into the interstate network of the world system. New areas are usually incorporated when the world economy goes through a period of restructuring as a part of its movement from phases of contraction to expansion. In this way, the links that bind an external area to the world system become constitutive of the latter's widened reproduction. The contents of these links vary depending on a whole array of configurations that characterize the world economy at the time of incorporation. They may involve the procurement or absorption of certain raw materials or commodities; an area that was hitherto external may become a supplier or receiver of population or labor; or such an area can become strategically important for the interstate system. Whatever their contents, these links undermine the preincorporation networks in the area. Once they are established, they irrevocably bind the incorporated area to the global system, and as a result this area ceases to be a proper historical unit by itself.

Peripheralization

Starting with incorporation, the form, content, and consequences of the processes that determine the relative status of a zone in the world economy depend on (a) the geographical characteristics and natural endowments of the region; (b) historically specific conditions that prevailed in the region prior to incorporation and the way in which these became transformed during incorporation; and (c) the particular phases and stages which the capitalist world economy moves through in this time period. In conjunction with these three shaping conditions, a broad social transformation takes place in an incorporated region. In the course of this transformation there is no simple direction (incline or decline) to social change. Many existing groups and relations die out, many new groups and relations develop, but most of all existing groups in relation to one another are transformed. Various groups with conflicting interests are necessarily involved at various points of this process, and it is true that the ascent of one group or sector almost always takes place at the expense of one or more others. As a concomitant of this social transformation, the incorporated region comes to occupy a structurally and historically determined position within the axial division of labor and the interstate system of the capitalist world economy. Peripherality is one of these positions. In general it involves a relation of subordination to other centers of accumulation (i.e., to the core and semiperipheral areas). But the substance of the relations that define a peripheral area and the type of economic activities that concentrate there vary from one historical period to the other.

CONTOURS OF THIS STUDY

Trade as a Mediating Process

The incorporation of the Ottoman Empire was achieved mainly through the mediation of trading activities that linked the sites of agricultural production in, especially, the Balkans and Western Anatolia with the processes of production and/or household consumption elsewhere in the world economy, especially in core areas. During the second half of the nineteenth century some foreign capital was invested in government loans, public utilities, and infrastructure that was related to trade. Little of this went directly to agriculture or industry. In other words, during peripheralization, trade continued to be the main link between the Ottoman Empire and the capitalist world economy. Accordingly, the following analysis of the growing interrelatedness between the empire and the world economy is centered primarily on trade.

Western Anatolia as an Area of Concentration

Western Anatolia was an important region for the provisioning of the imperial centers during the classical age of the Ottoman Empire. It was also one of the first areas, along with the Balkans, to be integrated into global networks. But unlike the Balkans, Western Anatolia formally remained a part of the Ottoman Empire as well as the new Turkish Republic throughout the nineteenth century and after. This region thus constitutes an appropriate site where the transformation of the redistributive networks and that of social hierarchies can be examined during peripheralization.

Mid-Nineteenth Century as a Focus

During the classical period, markets in the Ottoman Empire were either completely subordinated to the political priorities of the ruling class and were administered by them, or the independent relations of exchange were too marginal to support an alternative order to the one dominated by the Ottoman ruling class. By the middle decades of the nineteenth century this situation had changed. Then, market exchange and political domination existed as separate and equally powerful processes competing with each other to integrate the Ottoman social structures. Toward the end of the nineteenth century, the bureaucratic class once again dominated the social and economic processes in the empire. However, by this period not only had world historical conditions changed but the imperial apparatus and the nature of the markets in the empire had also undergone substantial transformation. As a result of these changes, bureaucrats had acquired economic as well as political purposes in regulating the Ottoman economy. In other words, the type of domination they exercised later in the century was substantively different from the one they had access to prior to the nineteenth century. The separation between the state and economy (or markets in particular) originated with the incorporation of the Ottoman Empire into the capitalist world economy and the development of the relationship between these two spheres was one of the principal factors that underlay the peripheralization of the Ottoman Empire during the nineteenth century. Therefore, the middle decades of that century—when the political processes and market exchange became equally plausible, historical alternatives for the future integration of Ottoman social structures—constitutes the main temporal focus of this work.

Chapter Outline

The three main chapters of this study follow a chronological order. Chapter Two starts with a brief review of the nature and consequences of the interaction between the European economy and the Ottoman Empire in the sixteenth century. This is followed by a depiction of the incorporation of the Ottoman Empire into the world economy between ca. 1750 and 1815 and the concomitant transformation of the Ottoman social structures.

At the end of incorporation, the Ottoman Empire was closer to occupying an intermediate (i.e., semiperipheral) position within the world economy. But its fortunes were reversed, and the imperial social structures were progressively peripheralized in the course of the nineteenth century. This reversal is explained in Chapter Three by focusing on its three main determinants. These are, first, the way in which the world economy was restructured after the end of the Napoleonic wars; second, the substantive weakness of the Ottoman state, which was evident in its fundamental inability to acquire or develop effective means of controlling the economic and social processes; and third, the structure of local networks that had developed during incorporation which are described within the context of western Anatolia.

Chapter Four shows how the dominant groups of these networks seized the favorable conditions of the mid-nineteenth century and enhanced their already advantageous position in the local social matrixes. They organized and supported the expansion of commodity production and trade in western Anatolian agriculture. By virtue of their strategic position in these networks, they were able to appropriate most of the new wealth that was generated through the expanded economic activity. The results of the mode of appropriation of this wealth were such that regionally, the cleavage between the coastal and inner areas widened to the benefit of the former; socially, the classical hierarchies were overturned with the Muslim potentates becoming dependent on and subordinate to the non-Muslim merchants and bankers of the region. On the bases of the patterning of these networks and the type of interrelatedness they came to exhibit with the global networks, I characterize their development as an aspect of the peripheralization of the Ottoman Empire.

After touching upon some of the changes that occurred in world historical conditions during the late nineteenth century, and their relationship to Ottoman social structures, the book ends with a series of inferences about social change in a peripheral area such as the Ottoman Empire.

Sources

As primary material, this work relies extensively on the various reports and evaluations written by the representatives of foreign governments and by other foreigners who were living or traveling in the Ottoman Empire during those years. In some ways, this has limited the general perspective of this study to a European viewpoint. In order to correct this bias, an attempt was made to consult the records of the sharia courts in İzmir.[8] These records provide a diverse and rich source of information for analyzing the social substance of the transformation of the Ottoman Empire during the nineteenth century. But in this study they could be used only in a limited way, because the İzmir collection did not lend itself to the long-term analysis of the economic matters. It is hoped that in the future the use of such records, along with other private material and the kind of documents used here, will substantiate further the general framework and interpretation offered in this book. The study of such records and their use in projects like this one should be seen as constitutive of a total history. They should be compared with documents of other types, with others of the same type, and with accounts that represent different angles. Since each one of these will pertain to a particular appraisal of a specific situation, comparing them will help bring forth salient discontents, disagreements, divisions, and contradictions within the Ottoman society. When placed in a broad theoretical and historical framework, such opposing tendencies will facilitate our understanding of the dynamics of social change in the Ottoman Empire. Then, we can see that the use of documents that have temporally and geographically limited viewpoint is not incompatible with our macroconcerns or with our understanding of historical sociology as a futurist and critical science that pertains to the totality of human experience.

2

From Two Worlds to One: The Ottoman Empire and the Capitalist World Economy

The classical system of the Ottoman Empire is usually characterized on the basis of the key imperial institutions as they existed in the sixteenth century.[1] This is not surprising, since it was only during that century that the empire reached a certain degree of stability. For two hundred years before that time, imperial institutions—more importantly, the relationships and processes that were embodied in them—had been in continuous development. Yet, if we move some one hundred years past the sixteenth century, we find that few if any of the classical characteristics remained intact for long. Starting from precisely the moment of apex in the "golden age," a cascade of modifications and innovations were introduced by the Ottoman government in the areas of administration, taxation, military mobilization, and economic control within the empire. It may be suggested that what we see in either side of this divide is essentially the same state of flux that characterized the entire history of the Ottoman Empire. Such an assertion would be useful as a corrective to the commonly held perception of the Ottoman Empire that denies it any dynamism whatsoever. Nevertheless, this should not lead us to overlook the difference in the kind and consequences of changes that took place before and after the sixteenth century. In the earlier period, institutional change was an aspect of the growth of the

11

empire. Through it, the central bureaucracy effectively integrated the Ottoman Empire as a social, political, and economic system. In the latter period, except for limited intervals, the successive interventions of the central government fell short of adequately dealing with the new reality of stagnant-to-shrinking territories and growing fiscal problems.

This moment of reversal in the historical trajectory of the Ottoman Empire coincides with some far-reaching transformations in Europe. Chief among these was the definitive shifting of the center of gravity of European trade from the Mediterranean to the Atlantic in the sixteenth century. As part of this realignment, the northwestern corner of the continent became the core of the nascent world economy.[2] This raises a number of questions regarding the nature and impact of the interactions between these two historical systems during this early period.[3] The key issue here pertains to the degree to which the Ottoman territories became an integral part of the division of labor of the world economy starting from as early as the sixteenth century.

We know that the population of the Ottoman Empire was increasing at an accelerated pace during the sixteenth century.[4] This brought additional pressure on the Ottoman resources which had already stopped expanding in absolute terms. The effects of these developments were accentuated by the flow of American silver into the Near Eastern markets.[5] Together they led to an inflationary period which shook Ottoman finances between 1556 and 1625.[6] In all these respects, the rhythm and direction of Ottoman trends conform to their European counterparts. We also know that Ottoman wheat exports to Europe increased notably in the sixteenth century, and that this was a period of rising wheat prices both in the Ottoman Empire and in Europe.[7] Are these facts sufficient for maintaining that the Ottoman Empire, at least in part, had become integrated into the world economy in this period?

To take the grain trade first, this was initially largely a contraband trade; but subsequently, high-ranking Ottoman officials both on the local and central levels participated in and profited from it. Even the holders of prebendal grants (*timar*) could sell a part of the tithe they were collecting in kind and benefit from favorable market conditions after fulfilling their government obligations.[8] It has been shown that the Balkan peasantry also was left with enough produce that they could market themselves after paying their taxes.[9] In other words, for the most part, Ottoman grain trade in the sixteenth century enriched the potentates of the classical system without undermining either the classical power relations or the position of the peasantry. Only if this trade had generated long-term gains for groups outside the purview of the central government could we discuss the possibility of a structural change resulting from the economic relations between the Ottoman Empire and Europe during this period.[10] But a long-term perspective shows that this was not the case. To the extent that one can talk about the beginnings of commercial agriculture outside of the immediate control of the central bureaucracy in the sixteenth century, this should be taken as a brief and limited phenomenon rather than a long-term trend signaling the incorporation of the Ottoman Empire into the world system.[11] Toward the end of the sixteenth century, when grain exports started to threaten the system of provisioning, the central government was able to initiate a meticulous policy of control, successfully curbing both official and contraband forms of wheat trade. After the turn of the seventeenth century, political control of the Ottoman wheat trade was made easier by the contraction of the world economy. Declining wheat prices was one aspect of that period which presumably rendered the risks of contraband not worth taking.[12]

WEAKENING OF THE IMPERIAL APPARATUS: SEVENTEENTH AND EIGHTEENTH CENTURIES

Control Over Production

During the rest of the seventeenth and eighteenth centuries, the bureaucrats were occasionally successful in combating their fiscal and administrative problems; but generally, continuing contraction of revenue sources forced them to opt for *ad hoc* methods that were likely to generate quick results. In agriculture, the timar system was abandoned in favor of an expanded version of tax farming and different types of leasing arrangements for life.[13] This led to the dispersal of the claims of ownership and possession over land and to the blurring of the lines of responsibility toward the central government. It was no longer easy for the central bureaucrats to keep track in an adequate manner of who had how much right over which property.[14] The spread of tax farming also made it difficult for the bureaucrats to maintain a direct contact with the producers. Peasants were now confronted with the subcontractors of tax farmers whose main interest was in maximizing their returns as quickly as possible so that they could pay off debts and renew contracts. In relating to the direct producers, the tax farmer or his agent was at total liberty to use a multitude of means to realize his objective, and peasants no longer had any way of acquiring real protection against these.[15] Establishment of de facto peasant proprietorship and the abuse of tax-exempt pious foundations (*waqf* institution) constituted two other channels through which the control of land was gradually wrested from the government after the sixteenth century in various regions of the Ottoman Empire.[16] Whatever the particular method, the end result was the same in that the lessee, the owner, the waqf administrator, or, in some cases, the peasant was in a position to organize production and alter the kind, volume, and direction of activities originating from his holdings without any interference by the government.[17] In other words, central government was losing its ability to supervise agriculture, the largest and the most important sector of the imperial economy.

Starting from the seventeenth century, the Ottoman government became less and less able to control production in urban manufactures as well. In particular, three factors worked to the detriment of Ottoman guilds in which most of the urban manufacture was organized. These were, first, the government's inability to provide monetary stability; second, the movement of large numbers of poor peasants in to the cities; and third, the economic exhaustion caused by the long wars of the seventeenth century which undermined the dependability of the urban markets.[18] Traditionally, the government had utilized the guild hierarchy to collect taxes from the artisan class.[19] Therefore, as these organizations lost their strength, the central government moved to auction various administrative posts of the guilds in a manner and with consequences that were similar to those of tax farming in agriculture. This general picture of the Ottoman guilds must be qualified with two further observations. First, a substantial part of manufacturing activity in the Ottoman Empire took place in rural areas. While important for local subsistence, these did not constitute a source of revenue for the Ottoman government. Neither were they influenced directly by the developments that affected the urban manufactures before the nineteenth century.[20] Second, as they became less burdened by politically formulated restrictions, manufacturing activities such as cotton weaving in the Balkans and in Anatolia, wool in Salonika, and silk in Bursa experienced intermittent growth in the course of the seventeenth and eighteenth centuries.[21] In terms of its long-term consequences, this was an important development. Not only was the government not able to tax or control such flourishing lines of manufacture, but they also opened up the possibility of private accumulation of wealth and power by the larger producers in such guilds.

Control Over the Means of Administration and Violence

As central control over production and taxation became less and less effective, provincial administrators and other local figures found new ways of expanding their power and influence.[22] This tendency became widespread especially among the wealthy local notables (*ayan*) who had traditionally acted as the representatives of townspeople in their dealings with the government.[23] In the seventeenth and the eighteenth centuries, the central government, in an effort to integrate these people into the administrative apparatus, appointed some of them as tax collectors (*muhassıls*) and as administrators of bureaucrat's estates (*mütesellim*).[24] But contrary to the bureaucrats' expectations, such titles enhanced the legitimacy of the power and influence of the ayan. At the same time, but independently from this development, both the ayan and government officials were becoming tax farmers. Consequently, the close correspondence between the size, revenue, and location of the prebendal grants and the authority that was vested in a particular governmental position started to disappear.[25] Ayan were in a better position to take advantage of administrative laxity because of their long-term familiarity with their regions. Government officials, on the other hand, were becoming less secure in their tenure. To make the most of their typically brief appointments, they resorted to venality and nepotism, and borrowed at exorbitant rates to meet their expenses.[26] While the central bureaucrats could keep their representatives under some semblance of control through frequent rotation and by playing different officials against each other, there was little they could do to curb the expanding power and influence of the ayan. Moreover, government was becoming dependent on these very usurpers of its authority for the collection of taxes, maintenance of order, and the raising of auxiliary troops.[27]

One of the most important factors that contributed to the rise of the provincial notables and other peripheral elements of the Ottoman Empire was their newly acquired access to standing troops and to means of violence. This represented a radical departure from the way in which the Ottoman army was organized and from the regulations on weapons within the classical system. The centralized administration and the methods of recruitment of the Ottoman army had provided the empire with a clear edge over feudal Europe for three centuries. From the seventeenth century onward, however, the new and stronger states of Europe that were equipped with advanced military techniques started to challenge Ottoman superiority effectively. The obsolescence of the Ottoman military apparatus became apparent during the long and inconclusive wars with Austria between 1593 and 1606. As a remedy, the central government ordered the provincial officials to form mercenary units and equip them with firearms. Shortly thereafter, the number of Janissaries was increased from thirteen thousand in the 1550s to thirty-eight thousand in the 1600s. Both of these measures were meant to provide temporary supplements to the prebendal (*timarlı*) army, many of whose members were refusing to use muskets,[28] but they sowed the first seeds of radical change in the Ottoman military organization. In contrast to the classical army, most of whose troops would be disbanded at the end of a campaign, mercenaries remained organized in their companies at times of peace as well. They were ready and willing to provide their services to whomever hired them. During the long intervals of peace in the eighteenth century (such as 1718–36, 1739–68, 1774–87, 1792–98), local notables retained the mercenary troops to back their challenges against the central government.[29] When unemployed, these *sekban* troops became a menace to rural order; they practiced brigandage on their own, and demanded illegal dues and protection money from the peasants.[30] On the other hand, the large number of people who were recruited to the Janissary army lacked proper fighting skills. The government was not able to provide for their training, nor did the treasury have sufficient funds to pay their salaries regularly. To provide for themselves, Janissaries acquired various trades and, in violation of their traditional code of professionalism, infiltrated or forcefully entered the craft guilds. Also, their presence in increasingly large numbers in the major cities of the Ottoman Empire made them a political force to be reckoned with.[31] One important outcome of these developments was that they undermined the legitimacy of the Ottoman government in the eyes of its subjects. Having lost the multifarious checks and balances that were at their disposal under the classical system, the government officials themselves resorted to force to keep societal divisions intact. Reaya was burdened with increasingly oppressive taxes; rural uprisings of the seventeenth century were suppressed with extreme ferocity; and peasants and nomads were forcefully deported and resettled in an effort to maintain the agricultural base of society.

The loosening of government control over the production, administration, and the means of violence, was bound to have a regressive effect on the ability of the central bureaucracy to supervise the circulation of commodities and capital, especially across the imperial borders. However, there was no significant change in this latter aspect until the middle decades of the eighteenth century. The structure of the Ottoman Empire was not conducive to the reorientation of trade channels in the direction of creating new marketing networks. Exchange networks in the Ottoman Empire were organized around the major urban centers; the most important of these was centered in Istanbul, and extended into the core provinces of the empire.[32] While it is evident that after the sixteenth century the Ottoman government was increasingly unable to control the activities of the carriers of these trades, local and long-distance merchants did not have any immediate reason for rerouting their activities away from Istanbul and other urban centers. Furthermore, after its first long wave of expansion, the world economy itself went through a prolonged period of contraction that was especially manifest in the declining grain prices between the seventeenth and the mid-eighteenth centuries.[33] Mercantilist policies that the European states adopted to protect themselves further depressed European markets, and this made trade with Europe even less attractive for Ottoman merchants.

The world economic and political conjuncture during the early eighteenth century even permitted the Ottomans to embark upon a fairly important, albeit shortlived, reorganization of their economy. Existing branches of manufacture such as cotton, wool, and silk weaving expanded in various provinces of the empire, and new lines of manufacturing activity, such as iron smelting in the Balkans and soap making in Crete, were established.[34] Most of these industries were actively supported or in some instances directly set up by the government. They obtained most of their raw materials from domestic sources and for the most part produced for Ottoman markets, where the major purchaser was the government itself.

Brief rejuvenations such as this one notwithstanding, by the eighteenth century the Ottoman Empire had digressed significantly from the formal and substantive principles of its classical organization. Thus, at the end of the eighteenth century the Ottoman Empire was less centralized, less strong, and, therefore, more open to outside pressures than it was in the sixteenth century. In this sense, it is appropriate to mark the sixteenth century as some kind of turning point in the annals of Ottoman history. But the key to this inflection should be sought not in some internal decay but in major changes that took place in the (external) conditions of existence of the Ottoman Empire. In particular, there was the fact that the empire had reached the limits of its territorial expansion. Any major gain against the European states was proved impossible; the desert territory to the south made a natural barrier; and eastward expansion was precluded because the Ottomans had incorporated the provinces in this part of the Empire only in a very loose manner in the first place.

Secondly, the difficulties of raising sufficient revenue were multiplied as a result of the shifting of trade routes toward the Atlantic, which put an end to the central importance of the Mediterranean in world trade. The Ottoman government could no longer count on transit trade as a source of revenue for its coffers. Looked at in this perspective, it appears that some of the difficulties of the Ottomans between the sixteenth and eighteenth centuries were caused more by the exclusion of their empire from the hub of the new capitalist order than its incorporation into this growing network.

After the middle decades of the eighteenth century, world economic and political trends changed in important ways, generating a strong pull that affected primarily the western provinces of the Ottoman Empire. The field of attraction that developed in Europe had three major constituents: (1) the cyclical upturn in grain prices, (2) the increased demand generated for goods by the newly developing industries of Europe, and (3) the almost uninterrupted succession of wars and revolutions of the late eighteenth century that created immense opportunities for contraband and speculative profiteering. Individually and together, these factors created a strong incentive for Ottoman merchants to reroute their trade away from imperial centers and toward European markets, a process against which the Ottoman government had been left with little means of resisting.

PROCESSES OF INCORPORATION (1750–1815)

Circulation of Goods, People, and Money

Initially, contraband trade in grains, especially wheat, constituted the most important link between the Balkan provinces and the European markets. It was primarily the increasing prices in Europe that prompted Ottoman merchants to smuggle this most jealously guarded article of the imperial system out of the Ottoman Empire. For example, between 1780 and 1813 the price of wheat in Salonika increased almost fourfold, from twelve *gurush* per *kile* to forty-five.[35] Because of its very nature it is difficult to determine the volume of contraband trade. According to some estimates, during the second half of the eighteenth century approximately 40% of the grain production of Macedonia and Thessaly was exported.[36] The main carriers of contraband grain from the Thessalian, Macedonian, and the western Anatolian littorals and from the Hungarian plains were the Greek shippers and merchants. In the last quarter of the eighteenth century, these Greek carriers were traveling as far as France and Spain, and some of them even crossed the Atlantic.[37] It is worth noting that contraband trade was flourishing at a time when the Ottoman government was trying to stiffen its provisioning demands from the western provinces because Egyptian grains were becoming less and less available owing to the political problems there.[38] Often the officials who were charged with implementing government orders became the willing accomplices in these ventures for their personal enrichment.[39] As a result of the increasing shortages in basic necessities, the prices of all the major commodities increased significantly during the second half of the eighteenth century. For example, between 1779 and 1800 in Istanbul, the price of bread increased from five *para/okka* to twelve; that of barley from fifteen para/okka in 1756 to sixty para/okka in 1800; and lamb from ten para/okka to twenty-four para/okka during the same years.[40]

During the second half of the eighteenth century, contraband trade in grains was joined by the export of commercial crops such as cotton, maize, tobacco, grapes, livestock, and commercial fibers. In every commodity, the growing demand from developing industries of central and western Europe was the prime factor that made the expansion (or, the introduction, as in maize)[41] of these crops' cultivation possible.[42] Cotton cultivation in Macedonia and western Anatolia expanded three times between 1720 and 1800, and most of the output was destined for export.[43] At the high point of its cultivation, in the last years of the eighteenth century, cotton was fetching twice the price of grain in Salonika.[44] Development of livestock raising in Serbia was closely related to the reversion of the Hungarian, Slovenian, and Banat lands to grain from animal husbandry. In a short period of time Serbia was able to replace Hungary as the major supplier of pigs to central European markets. Between 1777 and 1786, Hungary imported about 1.3 million francs worth of pigs from the Ottoman Empire, mostly from Serbia; and by the 1800s Serbia was exporting annually 3 million francs worth of pigs and cattle to Austria.[45]

The two most important direct customers of Ottoman exports were the French and the Austrians. It is estimated that between 1786 and 1789, 83% of the total imports of France were coming from the Levant, and that cotton constituted 70% of these imports.[46] Austrian trade increased after the opening of the Danube and was aided by the Habsburg policy of promoting Austro-Balkan trade.[47] Between 1741 and 1747, the Ottomans were exporting annually an average of three million florins worth of goods to Austria; but in 1778 this figure had gone up to nine million.[48] Included in these figures was the Ottoman exports to Saxony,

Switzerland, and Prussia, for all of which Austria was the main intermediary of the Levant trade.

Interstate relations constitute the third factor that determined the
expansion of Ottoman trade with Europe in the late eighteenth century.
To begin with, relatively long periods of peace between the Ottomans
and the Austrians were responsible for the development and security
of overland routes in east central Europe, providing safe passage of
goods and people across the borders of the two empires.[49] The real
impetus to Ottoman trade, however, came from the wars and revolutions
of the late eighteenth century that created new opportunities for Ottoman
producers and merchants. For example, the effects of the American and
French revolutions on global trade in cotton and cotton textiles were
the major factors behind the first cotton boom in the western provinces
of the Ottoman Empire.[50] The Ottomans were not directly involved in
the War of the Austrian Succession or the Seven Years War and were
only briefly entagled in the Napoleonic Wars. But along with the French
Revolution, the rapid succession of these conflagrations in Europe forced
the major maritime powers of Europe (especially France) to withdraw
from the eastern Mediterranean. The vacuum was filled by the Greek
merchant shippers, who quickly became the major carriers of contraband
and official Ottoman trade. The difficulty of policing the seas under war
conditions further curtailed the government's ability to control the
movement of commodities in and about the empire, making contraband
ventures easier.[51] In this respect, the continental blockade that was
imposed by Napoleon and the British counterblockade proved to be
particularly beneficial for Ottoman merchants. By taking advantage of
Austrian acquiescence, they carried both the lucrative British contraband
trade and Balkan grain and other Ottoman products into central Europe.[52]
Two major wars in which the Ottomans fought with the Russians
(1768–74 and 1787–92) ended the exclusive control of the Black Sea
and the Danube by the Ottomans. As a result, Istanbul was gradually
reduced from a major center of trade where foreign ships had to transport
their cargoes to and from the Black Sea to a mere port of call. Not
only was the treasury losing revenue but the Danube and the Straits
were becoming extraverted conduits of trade, leading to further difficulties in the adequate provisioning of the city.[53]

Several migrations that took place within and across Ottoman territories during the last quarter of the eighteenth century provided the
social fabric for the economic networks that were developing in the
border regions of the Ottoman Empire. The most important among
these was the spread of Greeks into all the major commercial areas of

the Balkans, strengthening their historically privileged position in the foreign trade of the empire. Greeks were aided in this by the political power that the Greek patriarchate had acquired in Istanbul. Also, with the emigration of the Jewish population to Europe and to western Anatolia, the Greeks were freed from one of their most formidable rivals in the Balkan trade.[54] The movement of the Greek population was not confined to Ottoman territories. Many were drawn into Russia and Austria by the active policies of these governments to attract non-Muslim and non-Turkish groups into their borderline provinces. This human connection with Austrian and Russian lands became important, especially after the opening of the Black Sea and the Danube to international navigation in 1774.[55] Greek merchants also established themselves in the major commercial centers of Europe such as Vienna, Leipzig, Paris, Marseilles, and London.[56] The network that was developing was such that, for example, a Chiean family like the Rallis had members in the major cities in Europe as well as in the Balkans.[57]

The demographic composition of the Balkans was further altered by the movements of the Vlachs, who were fleeing from Albanian mercenaries and the local ayan. Starting from Moskopol on the Greek-Albanian border, they moved first to Salonika and then north to the Habsburg border town of Zemun in the 1770s.[58] After settling there, the Vlachs became prominent intermediaries in the livestock trade between the Ottoman Empire and Austria. Similarly, Bulgarian peasants who were escaping in the 1790s from the forces of the Albanian ayans moved north to Wallachian towns. There they provided artisan labor for Bulgarian merchants, especially in Bucharest and Giurgiu.[59] Rural disorder caused by the rebellious ayan and irregular troops also forced a large number of Serbian peasants to move into the mountains, where they became engaged in the raising and wholesale trade of livestock, especially pigs.[60]

These population movements created a substantive basis for the expansion of trade across the western borders of the Ottoman Empire. The settlements of the Vlachs and Greeks intersected Austrian, Ottoman, and Russian territories, and greatly facilitated the rerouting of the region's commercial arteries. The nationalities of these intermediaries varied, but their specialization was the same in that they were all engaged in "bringing goods in and out of the Ottoman Empire."[61] In other words, these settlements created a human fabric through which goods were easily diverted away from Istanbul. Also, rural disorders that were responsible for much of the peasant displacement soon reached Balkan cities. Major centers such as Belgrade, were frequently attacked and sacked by the

Albanian and Turkish ayan. The urban population, like their rural counterparts, had to leave their occupations and flee either to the mountains or across the border to Austria and Russia. The result was a relative decline in Balkan population that, by undermining agricultural production and urban manufactures, further limited the government's ability to generate revenue and maintain its provisioning policy.[62] Finally, the population movements of the late eighteenth century served to recast the ethnic composition in the Balkans. Within the area as a whole, the population tended to concentrate in northwestern zones, particularly in the towns. The proportion of the Muslim component decreased in a gradient from the east to the west.[63] In Stoianovich's words, the Balkan towns were becoming "less Jewish, less Armenian, less Turkish, and more Greek, more Slavic and more Albanian."[64] In long-term effects, population movements of the eighteenth century constituted the first steps toward the realization of the yet distant goal of uninational towns and uninational states.[65]

Emerging networks in the Balkans were detrimental to the imperial system not only because they mediated the diversion of goods away from the imperial centers but also because they effectively blocked the transmission of cash revenues from these wealthiest provinces to the capital. In the absence of control over their activities, merchants, tax farmers and their associates acquired new means of keeping and using the taxes they were collecting for their own benefit. As the government's fiscal problems deepened, the bureaucrats tried to affect a redistribution of the shrinking revenues by channeling a greater part of it toward the central treasury and away from the prebendal areas and the Sultan's private purse. Expanding the scope of tax farming—including new and bigger sources of revenue into life-long leasing arrangements—and instituting extraordinary taxes in order to appropriate part of the private fortunes of higher bureaucrats and wealthy individuals were the most readily available means of achieving such a transfer of revenues.[66] While each one of these policies generated short-term or one-time increases in revenue, none could be the solution to the fiscal problems of the Ottoman state in the long run. In fact, for the most part, by enhancing the importance of tax farmers and their financiers, these interventions reinforced precisely the decentralizing tendencies which the central government was trying to combat. At least in theory, embarking on a sustained policy of supporting production and trade was the only alternative that could lead to a real expansion in revenues. However, such an option could be adopted only within the framework of a long-term undertaking which was difficult to conceive in the face of the growing budgetary pressures. As for borrowing from abroad, there were some muted suggestions for taking such a route as early as the 1780s; but they did not materialize, as this had not yet become an acceptable option.[67] Beyond these, the bureaucrats had one more way of attempting to deal with the immediate problem of covering the deficits. This was to debase the coinage, to which they resorted with increasing frequency after the late eighteenth century.[68]

On the one hand, this de facto devaluation made the Ottoman exports cheaper and made it even easier for the merchants to find markets for Ottoman goods. But on the other hand, debasements threw the Ottoman monetary system into absolute chaos. By decreasing the silver content of currency, bureaucrats had hoped to use the silver that was thus saved to meet their external obligations. However, debasement of coins fueled inflationary trends at home and led to the steady decline of the value of Ottoman monies in European markets. Consequently, it became even more difficult for the Ottoman government to meet these obligations.[69] Within the empire, the same coins had acquired different values in different places, which made interregional trade extremely difficult to plan or conduct on a long-term basis.[70]

Upon realizing that the government was dispensing debased coins, prominent merchants who had access to good currency, and to gold and silver, hoarded them to use in their private transactions or sent them abroad through the conduits provided by the new commercial networks.[71] Liquid capital was already scarce in the empire and this made the situation even worse. Consequently, lending money at exorbitant rates to all sections of society, including tax farmers, provincial governors, bureaucrats, and peasants, became a profitable area of investment for these merchants.

New Forms of Labor Control

The accelerated circulation of goods, people, and money constitute the formal indicators of the intensifying relations between the Ottoman Empire and the world economy. But it was the underlying transformation in the social and economic spheres that vested these formal links with a substantively different character and set this period apart from previous phases of expansion in Ottoman foreign trade.

In the rural parts of the Balkans and western Anatolia, the changes that took place in the production processes can best be depicted in the disappearance of the classical prebendal system and its effective replacement by *çiftlik* agriculture. In urban manufactures, the situation was one of protracted stagnation for most of the eighteenth and early nineteenth centuries. Depending on their locality and on the prevailing conditions, however, some branches of production could expand their activities by supplying more distant regions and some of the requisitions of the government, especially for army needs. Cotton cloth production in Ambelikia and coarse cotton production in Plovdiv are among the best known examples of this latter category.[72] But success stories such as these were rare and limited to particular conjunctures. Therefore, our main focus here will be on agriculture, where some fundamental changes took place in the late eighteenth century.

Çiftlik agriculture differed from the classical system of land use in two major ways.[73] First, unlike the prebendal class, whose claim on land and on its products was based on the power that had been delegated to it by the government, çiftlik owners were exercising de facto (if not de jure) rights of private property on land. Consequently, they were primarily motivated by their personal interest in maximizing their returns and protecting and improving their own social status. Second, the difference between the prebendal and çiftlik types relates to methods of cultivation and the mix of products grown on çiftliks. Especially toward the end of the eighteenth century, larger and larger parts of the çiftlik estates were devoted to the profitable crops of the period (such as cotton and maize) in the Balkans. The choice of the crop was largely dictated by market conditions, and it involved reorganization of the processes of production under the supervision of the çiftlik owner.

It is usually thought that the size of the çiftliks constituted a third factor that distinguished them from the previously prevalent types of agricultural production in the Ottoman Empire. A consensus was created by earlier scholarship that çiftliks were plantation-like estates similar to the large farms of eastern and central Europe that were developing contemporaneously.[74] Recent research on the topic has revised this perception by demonstrating that the majority of the çiftliks in the Balkans and western Anatolia were composed of smaller holdings.[75] For example, in the Manastir region in Macedonia, 75.7% of the çiftliks were found to be less than 58 hectares.[76] In Bulgarian, Greek, and Macedonian lands, the size of çiftliks varied from 30 to 500 hectares, but they were typically concentrated on the lower end of the spectrum.[77] In western Anatolia, the average size of the çiftliks could be as small as 90 hectares and as large as 734 hectares.[78] Compared with the Prussian and Polish estates of several thousand acres, çiftliks in the Ottoman Empire were indeed "no great affair."[79] Furthermore, some of the larger holdings were established during the classical period, as they were reclaimed from the waste and improved for cultivation by bureaucrats of higher echelons. As such, they were part of the classical system and cannot be seen as offshoots of the commercial developments of the late eighteenth century.[80]

Our primary interest lies not with the status of such lands but with the changes that took place in those that had been held as state property and distributed in small parcels as prebendal grants. It was the de facto conversion of these types of lands by competing ayans, armed irregulars, or the members of the old prebendal class, that signified a fundamental transformation in land tenure in the Ottoman Empire.

The most intense period of çiftlik formation on such properties corresponds to the late eighteenth century. This was a period of expansion in the world economy and, as such, one that offered enhanced marketing possibilities for Ottoman products in European markets.[81] The Ottoman government was no longer in a position to intervene in this process. Local officials, especially the *kadı*s, were often in collusion with the notables and other usurpers, and consequently the local courts were either unable or unwilling to adjudicate in çiftlik-related cases.[82] Furthermore, the spread of tax farming between the sixteenth and the eighteenth centuries had given semilegal status to the claims of the ayan and other groups who had become tax farmers themselves.[83] Under the conditions of spiraling fiscal and administrative anarchy, tax farmers, their agents and subcontractors, and the rural collectors of direct taxes found a multitude of bureaucratic loopholes and opportunities to enlarge their lands by usurping peasant households.

To take advantage of favorable market conditions, çiftlik owners had to make sure that they had enough laborers to work on the land, a task made somewhat easier by the conditions under which çiftliks were formed in the last quarter of the eighteenth century.[84] A high land/labor ratio continued to be a demographic trait of most of the Ottoman provinces, but widespread brigandage made it difficult for peasants to find safety if they were not under the protection of any of the competing forces. Nevertheless, when necessary, çiftlik owners did not hesitate to use forceful means to tie the peasants to their estates. For example, an ayan in the Serez region had five thousand armed guards in his service and used them for this purpose.[85] They also obtained special decrees from the government, permitting them to force peasants to return to land even if forty years had elapsed since their flight.[86] Çiftlik owners used force not only to restrict peasant mobility but also to impose the cultivation of new crops on their estates. For example, an ayan of the Bosna region beat his tenants to induce them to plant corn.[87]

A typical ciftlik estate that developed in the late eighteenth century consisted of a conglomeration of villages in which peasant households were still attending the plots of land they had received from the prebendal officers (*sipahi*) in previous decades. The major difference, however, was that now the peasants were "titularly" dispossessed.[88] On the average, 100 to 120 of such plots were converted into the private property of one of the contending families. Various means of coercion and conversion enabled çiftlik owners to coordinate and organize production on their estates. The major part of these çiftliks were usually devoted to the cultivation of a limited number of profitable crops of the period. Subsistence crops were grown and livestock was raised on the remaining part of the çiftlik property.[89]

For the average peasant household, the passage from the classical system to çiftlik agriculture involved a net deterioration in both economic and social terms. They often found themselves trapped in a vicious circle. The excessive demands on their labor and resources would occasionally prompt them to abandon their land, but they would soon discover that there was no place to go but to the estate of another çiftlik owner, and often under worse conditions. Peasant cultivators were now confronted with at least three sets of dues payable to three different entities. The classical taxes, including the regular tithe and the animal tax, were payable partly to the tax farmer and partly to the government officials. The old extraordinary taxes that the government had originally collected only in times of war or emergency (*avarız*) were now multiplied and made regular. Local administrators and provincial governors had instituted a whole series of new taxes (called *tekâlif-i şakka*) to augment their own incomes. Local ayan, armed irregulars, military chiefs, and religious leaders were also demanding payment of a multitude of irregular and illegal dues. Against the abuses that were inherent in all these demands, the peasants had no recourse, because the courts and other representatives of the central government were either unwilling or unable to intervene. Çiftlik formation had changed the status of the peasantry in their relationship to the production processes as well. They were transformed from being peasant producers whose freedom and protection was institutionally guaranteed to the status of, at best, sharecroppers—but more commonly, indebted tenants or dispossessed wage laborers.[90]

By the beginning of the nineteenth century, çiftlik agriculture had become the prevalent form of production in much of Thessaly, Epirus, Macedonia, Thrace, the Marica Valley, Danubian Bulgaria, Kosova, the Metobija Basin, the coastal plains of Albania, parts of Bosnia, and western Anatolia.[91] Almost all the export crops of the Ottoman Empire were drawn from these areas, and within them, çiftliks were especially concentrated around the main arteries of commerce and communication.[92]

However, in spite of the profitability of these crops, and despite the particular processes of production that entailed increased coercion and exploitation of the cultivators, çiftlik agriculture neither involved nor generated large-scale investments in Ottoman agriculture. There are several reasons for this. Whatever their background, çiftlik owners were almost invariably indebted to a relatively small number of private financiers who guaranteed the tax farming contracts, provided the çiftlik owners with the necessary resources to run their property, or organized the mercantile enterprises who purchased the product of these lands. Consequently, from its inception, the development of çiftlik agriculture was determined by the purely monetary interests of the financiers, who in turn imposed a framework that shaped the çiftlik owners' attitude toward farming and toward their estates. For the most part, they functioned as a group of town-dwelling absentee landlords whose main interest lay more with improving their own financial standing than in a long-term commitment to farming.[93] During the second half of the eighteenth century, when the government was particularly weak, they managed to keep their loosely integrated villages, and the development of favorable conditions in the European markets gave them a further opportunity to consolidate their positions. But at the same time, the abusive nature of their power provoked antagonism from the peasantry, who, in the Balkans, were mostly Christians—as opposed to the usurpers, who were mostly Muslims. Therefore, during the first decade of the nineteenth century, when the government was able to mobilize its army against the rebellious ayans, the local notables found little sympathy or support in their regions. Also, as marketing opportunities disappeared, financiers were divesting their funds from export trade and agriculture, and concentrating their efforts more and more in money lending and speculation. Çiftlik owners, who were losing the military edge they had acquired over the central government, were also being deprived of their financial support. In the end, they either suffered major defeats at the hands of the government forces and had their wealth and property confiscated, or they chose to seek better connections with the central bureaucracy. This reversal in the fortunes of the çiftlik owners opened the way for small peasantry to become, once again, the most prevalent form of production in Ottoman agriculture.

The Rise of Non-Muslim Intermediaries

After the late eighteenth century, the main beneficiaries of the expanding relations between the Ottoman Empire and the capitalist world economy were not the çiftlik owners or the government but commercial intermediaries.[94] Under the classical system, the policy of encouraging East-West trade through Ottoman territories, exclusion of foreign shipping from the Black Sea, total domination of the major overland routes between Europe and Asia, and the policy of provisioning, had given considerable importance to mercantile activity.[95] In the eastern provinces, Ottoman merchants who provided the link with Asian markets were predominantly Arab-Muslim and to a lesser extent Armenian; but among the merchant communities in the western provinces, non-Muslims—including Greeks, Armenians, Ragusans, and Jews—were more prominent than their Muslim counterparts.[96] The central bureaucracy could not administer the imperial system of provisioning without the participation of these intermediaries; but at the same time, the bureaucrats tried to set limits on the activities of these groups in order to prevent them from becoming independently powerful.[97] Consequently, over the years, local traders managed to stay in contact with the government, with local producers, and with foreign merchants simultaneously. From this position, they obtained a multitude of opportunities to derive personal benefits once the effectiveness of government control over production, administration, and circulation started to wane.

The specific rise of the non-Muslim merchants who were located in the western provinces occurred within the context of the growing importance of Ottoman-European trade after the eighteenth century and at a time when the strength of the imperial system was at a particularly low point.[98]

Starting from the middle decades of the eighteenth century, Greek merchants prevailed over the other non-Muslim groups, especially in the western trade of the Ottoman Empire. In addition to the increasing demand from Europe and the weakening of the central government, Greeks were aided by a number of additional factors in their ascent. They already had a numerical plurality in most of the Balkans, an advantage furthered by the particular patterns of migration in the eighteenth century. The Greeks of Istanbul were a positive factor in that they were the major bankers in the city, and they also dominated the Orthodox patriarchate. The Ottoman preference to administer the Orthodox millet through the Greek element helped expand the political and cultural influence of the Greek church in the Balkan provinces.[99]

Interstate politics that contributed to the expansion of Ottoman exports to Europe in the late eighteenth century were also an important factor in the rise of the non-Muslims, especially the Greek merchants in the western provinces of the Ottoman Empire. The opportunities for speculation and profiteering no doubt enhanced the position of the overland careers. But most significantly, these successive upheavals created a space for the Greek merchant marine to expand and, for a limited time, even monopolize shipping in the Aegean, Adriatic, Black Sea, and the eastern Mediterranean. The initial thrust of Greek shipping occurred when Greek corsairs were employed by the British to destroy French ships during the Seven Years War. The Russians resorted to the same method against the Ottomans during the wars of 1768–74 and 1787–92. When hostilities ceased, Greek sailors engaged in piracy and contraband trade, both of which helped them amass fortunes.[100] An important side growth of Greek shipping was the rise of the shipbuilding industry, especially on the Adriatic coast. Wealthy merchants of Patras and Janina made extensive investments in the dockyards of Galaxidi and Missolonghi and, according to some estimates, between 1786 and the eve of the Napoleonic Wars, the number of Greek ships increased from four hundred to one thousand.[101] The treaty of Küçük Kaynarca was doubly important for the Orthodox merchants of the Balkans. With this treaty, the Russian government obtained the right to represent and protect Orthodox subjects of the Ottoman Empire. Also, one of its most important clauses opened the Black Sea and, shortly thereafter, the Danube to international navigation. Russia did not have a merchant fleet in the Black Sea, so under provisions of the treaty, Ottoman Greeks hoisted the Russian flag and started to carry the trade of the southern provinces of the Russian Empire. Under this arrangement, Greeks were not only protected by the Russians, but were also enjoying the rights and privileges that were normally accorded only to foreign merchants in the Ottoman Empire. Muslims who had operated as merchants in the Black Sea region were unable to compete in the new mercantile networks.[102] Trade was not the only activity in which the local intermediaries became prominent. They were often the local agents of the tax farmers of Istanbul, subcontracted the tax farms themselves, and functioned as money lenders. Their versatility not only helped them multiply their fortunes but also allowed them to shift their resources among different alternatives. This latter aspect would become especially important in the long run, as it helped extend the intermediaries' influence beyond the limited periods of commercial expansion like that of the late eighteenth century.

After the end of the Napoleonic Wars, with the onset of yet another recession in the world economy, marketing opportunities for Ottoman products diminished. There are various indications that the intermediaries channeled some of the wealth which they accumulated through the commercial expansion of the late eighteenth century toward the secessionist movements in the course of the nineteenth century.[103] To cite a few examples, the first phase of the Serbian uprisings was led by Karageorge, who was a wealthy pig merchant.[104] The main ideological and organizational focus of the Greek revolution, Philiki Etairia, was formed by Greek merchants who had settled in Odessa,[105] and Greek fireships inflicted enormous losses on the Ottoman navy during the Morean uprisings of 1829.[106] Nevertheless, the relationship between mercantile interests as a whole and the crystalization of nationalist movements in the Balkans was not so straightforward. In spite of the numerical majority of the Greeks, Balkan merchants included a number of other groups, each with a different interest, and often in conflict with each other.[107] These diverse elements acted more or less in a complementary fashion as long as a propitious conjuncture in the European markets generated enough return to satisfy all the links of the network. But when contraction set in after the end of the Napoleonic Wars, and marketing opportunities for Ottoman products became limited, cleavages developed among the intermediaries. The groupings that developed did not always correspond to the ethno-religious categories of the classical system in that they often involved the redefinition of these categories, fracturing what had been assumed to be a fairly well-defined group. This last proposition can best be demonstrated in relation to the Greek plurality, whose relationship to the founding of the independent kingdom of Greece remained ambivalent throughout.[108] Given the large scope of their activities, the parceling of the Balkans among different states was likely to create obstacles to the movement of goods across the peninsula, and hence harm the interests of the larger of the Greek merchants especially.[109] On the other hand, in the face of shrinking markets, capitalizing on the gains of the previous decades by defining a political and national space was an attractive way of protecting the local mercantile interests against the other domestic or foreign merchants.

An exhaustive study of the growth, development and culmination of the nationalist movements in the Balkans would be beyond the scope of this chapter or this work in general.[110] Nevertheless, the economic contraction of the early nineteenth century highlighted some of the fundamental differences among a number of elements of the Balkan intermediaries, all of whom had benefited from the general processes that had incorporated the Ottoman Empire into the capitalist world economy. Generally, those concerns that were either based in Istanbul and other large cities, or those that were in close contact with such firms, increasingly adopted a conservative position, upholding the status quo and giving tacit support to the preservation of the Ottoman Empire in its weakened status. The more influential of the larger ayan, the owners of the larger çiftliks, and the higher echelons of the Phanariot aristocracy joined in with this group as well. The common thread that united these groups was that they were all profiting from the weakness of the central government. In line with their interests, the Orthodox patriarchate were especially vocal in denouncing Greek nationalists. In addition to their political influence, which would be threatened by the new kingdom, the Phanariots were also motivated by their own ideal of eventually revitalizing the Byzantine Empire within the entire territories of the Ottoman Empire, with Istanbul as the capital city.[111]

The support extended to the Ottoman government by the Istanbul-based *noblesse de robe* became more tangible as they became frequent bidders in tax-farming auctions, and creditors of the government treasury. Paralleling this shift of interest was the increasing frequency with which the local notables were succeeding in obtaining local and central posts within the bureaucratic apparatus. In the meantime, smaller local merchants, ethnic and religious leaders of the local communities, owners of the smaller çiftliks, and the peasantry were increasingly defining their interests locally and in opposition to this higher and broader realignment.[112]

Except for the Serbian uprising of 1804–18 and the Greek Revolution of 1829, the nationalist movements in the Balkans remained dormant for most of the late eighteenth and early nineteenth centuries, and did not come to real fruition until the last decades of the nineteenth century. The convergence of the formerly antagonistic forces on the level of the Ottoman state was an important factor that helped counteract the centrifugal forces that were taking root in the Ottoman Empire. This new trend reached a high point when some of the most prominent of the local notables signed a Pledge of Alliance in 1808, undermining the local configurations of power in an important way.[113] Through these developments, the Ottoman state, for the first time, was receiving support from a class outside the bureaucracy, and more significant, from a class that had established its prominence on the basis of extrapolitical processes. In the meantime the configuration of forces in the interstate system was developing in such a way as to put a premium on the preservation of the Ottoman state in its weakened posture. Consequently, domestic forces were soon joined by the European governments in propping up the Ottoman state.

The Ottoman State and the Interstate System

Formal ensconcing of the Ottoman state within the interstate system of the capitalist world economy can be traced through two developments: first, the changes in the nature and in the implications of the agreements that the Ottoman state entered into with European states after the middle decades of the eighteenth century; second, the institutional framework set up by the Ottomans to represent their interests abroad.

Starting with the treaties of Belgrade (1739) and Küçük Kaynarca (1774), diplomatic relations between the Ottoman Empire and the European states took a new turn.[114] The Treaty of Belgrade was concluded between the Ottoman and the Russian Empires with France acting as intermediary. In return for their services, the French demanded and received new privileges from the Ottoman Empire. Most significantly, the Ottoman government agreed to forego its stipulation that all capitulations must be renegotiated at the beginning of every new reign. In the aftermath of the Treaty of Belgrade, France broadened its political and economic influence and became the foremost European power in Near Eastern affairs. Other European powers, however, were quick to follow suit. Between 1739 and 1774 they, too, obtained the right to travel and trade under their own flags in Ottoman waters *except* in the Black Sea, the Danube, and the Straits. Mindful of these areas' importance for the provisioning of Istanbul, the Ottomans insisted that all goods, foreign and domestic, were to be carried into and out of these arteries of trade in Ottoman bottoms.[115] This stipulation was the last vestige of Ottoman control over these waters, a control that would completely disappear with the signing of the Küçük Kaynarca Treaty in 1774.

The Treaty of Küçük Kaynarca ended a six-year war between the Ottoman Empire and the Russians. With it, the Ottomans recognized the Russian acquisitions on the northern coast of the Black Sea, and conceded to the Russians freedom of navigation in all Ottoman waters, explicitly including the Black Sea, the Straits, and the Danube.[116] Russia thus became the only non-Ottoman power with extensive rights and privileges in the Black Sea, and obtained the opportunity to become firmly established in the Mediterranean. This threatened not only the European balance of power but also the individual interests of the European states. On the basis of the "most favored nation" clause in their capitulations, they exerted diplomatic pressure on the Ottoman government, which eventually agreed to recognize the similar rights of Austria in 1784, Britain in 1799, France in 1802, and Prussia in 1806.[117] Each of these signatory powers obtained also the right to extend the privileges arising from these treaties to "protected persons" in the Ottoman Empire, that is, to those who had ethnic or religious affiliation with the state in question. An Ottoman subject needed only to obtain a certificate from an ambassador or a consul to enjoy all the privileges that were accorded to foreign nationals. The main beneficiaries of these provisions were the non-Muslim merchants who had come to occupy a central position in the empire's foreign trade. Of course, this was but a new infringement on the capability of the Ottoman governments to control the circulation of commodities in and around the empire.[118] Finally, these treaties also provided foreign powers with new and effective means of interfering with the internal and external policies of the Ottoman state, which they would widely utilize in subsequent years.

Concomitant with the new treaties that were being signed with European states, the Ottoman government set up its first permanent embassies in London, Paris, Vienna, and Berlin. The intra-European problems of the early nineteenth century disrupted the growth of the Ottoman foreign service, but after the 1830s, the Ottoman Empire became well represented in all the major capitals of Europe and America. In addition to the embassies, a consular network was set up, covering North and South America, parts of Africa and Asia, as well as Europe.[119] Also, starting from the early nineteenth century, this global network was supported at home by a strengthened Translation Office. The title of the Chief Scribe (*Reis-ül Küttab*) was formally changed to Minister of Foreign Affairs, and he was put in charge of the Translation Office, which in effect became the seed of the Foreign Ministry. During the nineteenth century this office would become the most developed component of the Ottoman state apparatus, second only to the Interior Ministry in budgetary allocation.[120]

Throughout the third quarter of the eighteenth and the first decades of the nineteenth century, while Britain and France were trying to balance each other's political and economic gains in Ottoman territories, they were in unison in their efforts to neutralize the occasional advances in trade and diplomacy made by the Russians. Along with these powers, the subject nationalities of the Ottoman Empire tried to make the most out of the weakness of the Ottoman state. Thus, Napoleon occupied Egypt relatively easily in 1798 in his bid to challenge the British in the Far East; two wars with Russia (1768–74 and 1787–92) were followed by the first Serbian rebellion in 1804 and another war with Russia and the second Serbian uprising, both in 1812. The Wahabi rising in Arabia effectively constrained Ottoman authority there. The Greek revolution broke out in 1821. Yet a fourth war was fought with the Russians in 1828–29; and shortly thereafter, Egyptian Governor Muhammed Ali marched against the Ottoman army and threatened to take Istanbul itself. One way the Ottoman state managed to resist this multitude of attacks on its sovereignty was to use the interstate rivalry to its advantage. By actively seeking a defensive alliance with one of the powers, the Ottomans were often able to incite the others to join in and broaden the scope of the guarantees offered by that power. Also, in the face of the increasing seriousness of some of these attacks, and the financial burden which the wars entailed, it was becoming more and more clear to Ottoman bureaucrats that such treaty-bound commitments by the European states were becoming the only way in which the continuing existence of the Ottoman state could be secured.[121] Consequently, the successive alliances that the Ottoman state formed with European states at the turn of the nineteenth century became almost kaleidoscopic in character. In response to the French expedition in Egypt, a defensive pact was signed with Britain and Russia in 1799.[122] In 1806, shortly after they had renewed this pact with the Russians, the Serbian uprising forced the Ottomans to join in the continental war on the French side against their erstwhile allies.[123] In 1809, the 1799 treaty with Britain was renewed.[124] A few years later, Muhammed Ali's revolt brought another shuffling, because the French were inclined to support the governor and the British were slow in responding to Ottoman overtures for help. Thus the alliance with the Russians was strengthened with a comprehensive treaty of cooperation in 1833. On the basis of this treaty Russia sent in military aid and helped dispel the first phase of Muhammed Ali's attack on the Ottoman state.[125] The privileges that the Russians received in 1833 prompted the British to assume a more active role in Near Eastern affairs. A Treaty of Free Trade and Friendship was signed between the Ottomans and the British in 1838, and Britain played a central part in bringing the Egyptian problem to its definitive solution in the Straits Convention in London in 1841.[126]

The multilateral nature of these treaties and the widespread institutional support which they received gave a sense of permanency to the commitments of the Ottoman state in the interstate system. This was significantly different from the unilateral way in which the Ottomans perceived and interpreted their agreements with foreigners in the classical era.

CONCLUSION

The integration of the Ottoman state into the interstate system was the last step in the process of incorporation of the Ottoman Empire into the world economy. We have traced the beginnings of this process to the second half of the eighteenth century, when the commercial relations between the Ottoman Empire and Europe changed in several important ways: A growing portion of this trade was composed of an increasingly homogeneous group of cash crops that were in high demand in Europe; underpinning the rising trade between the western provinces of the Ottoman Empire and the core areas of the capitalist world economy was the transformation of the methods of production and forms of labor control in agriculture; and finally, the main beneficiaries of these expanding commercial relations were no longer the bureaucratic elite of the classical system but the non-Muslim traders in these regions and their private financiers and partners in Istanbul. On the basis of these substantive changes, I distinguish between the post-eighteenth and the earlier centuries, and argue that from the 1750s the western provinces of the Ottoman Empire were structurally integrated into the axial division of labor of the capitalist world economy. But these areas had been among the most important sources of supply for the provisioning of the capital city and other imperial metropoles. Their incorporation deprived the central government of substantial revenues and constituted a major blow to the redistributive system that was at the center of the classical organization of the Ottoman Empire. Already deprived of their classical pillars of strength, the bureaucrats made arrangements to utilize interstate diplomacy as the only remaining means of securing the survival of the Ottoman state in the world historical arena. On the bases of, first, the structural transformation that engulfed the imperial system in its entirety, and second, the integration of the Ottoman state into the interstate system, I argue that between ca. 1750 and ca. 1815 the Ottoman Empire as a whole was incorporated into the capitalist world economy.

3

After the Incorporation: 1815–1876

At the end of the period of incorporation, the Ottoman Empire was closer to occupying an intermediate position within the ambit of the world economy than being pushed to its periphery. During the Napoleonic Wars, total collapse of Anglo-European trade was avoided by the willingness of the Ottoman government and Ottoman merchants to relay British goods into central Europe. Also, on a more general level, and especially in the face of the increasing belligerency of the Russian Empire, Ottoman territories had the potential of becoming the most important link between the western European core and the peripheral zones in Asia. By the end of the Napoleonic Wars, the political weakening of the imperial structure had slowed down as a result of the support extended by local potentates and the European powers. Direct economic relations that were established between the various parts of the Empire and Europe during the late eighteenth century do not permit an easy classification of their status within the global division of labor either. Initially, wheat was the most important commodity exported by the Ottoman Empire, but this was largely through contraband trade and hence was subject to the vicissitudes of time and circumstances. Most of the trade in other goods that supplemented and eventually replaced

37

cereals was also conducted through illicit means, and in none of these did Ottoman territories have or acquire a competitive advantage. No commodity was exported in large enough quantities for a long enough time to provide a basis for delineating the status of the Ottoman Empire within the capitalist world economy. The assessment of the situation was even more difficult in relation to imports, because the domestic markets of the Ottoman Empire, especially those that were located in the interior, were not penetrated by European products until well into the 1820s. Consequently, much of the local production in urban and rural manufactures remained impervious to global trends. All of this makes it difficult to sustain an argument about the dependency of the local populace on the products of the metropolitan industries during these years.

If, on the other hand, we look at the Ottoman Empire from the vantage point of the 1870s, there would not be any basis for doubting its subordinate position within the global network of economic and political relations. The changes that had taken place in between were so significant that in 1879 Lord Derby, the British Foreign Secretary, confidently stated that "the daily surveillance of which [the Ottoman Empire] is the object in her domestic affairs has reduced her sovereign authority to practically zero."[1] A series of relations of power and hierarchies of production and exchange were established between the core areas of the capitalist world economy and the Ottoman Empire during the period that extended from the end of the Napoleonic Wars in about 1815 to the end of the mid-Victorian boom in about 1876; that is to say, it was in this period that the Ottoman Empire was peripheralized.

This chapter examines the three main determinants of this process. In general terms, these are identified as, first, those that related to the world economy where the relations of power and economic hierarchies were integrated and defined; second, Ottoman political structures as they related to the processes linking the empire with the world economy; and third, the local networks as they were permeated by and responded to the forces emanating from the loci of political and economic power in the world economy.

We will start by examining the reorganization of the global economic and political networks during the first three quarters of the nineteenth century, and then determine the place of the Ottoman territories within this changing configuration.

THE WORLD ECONOMY: 1815–1876

Contraction, 1815–1840

In the aftermath of the Napoleonic Wars, the foundations of the framework within which Britain had established her industrial strength was undermined from several directions. After the period of intense wars and revolutions, western European markets were no longer able to absorb the products of British industries on the levels that they had in the second half of the eighteenth century. Britain's access to these markets was further curtailed by the protective barriers that were erected by the European states in the postwar years. The gradual decline in the share of Europe in, for example, the export of cotton goods from England (from 60.1% in 1814–16 to 29.1% in 1854–56) came about as a result of these limitations and restrictions.[2] The mercantilist aura of the postwar years was not restricted to Europe. During the second quarter of the nineteenth century, as a result of the implementation of similar policies, the average annual surplus of about five million pounds, which had existed in Britain's trade with the United States and Canada, was replaced with an annual deficit of about six million pounds.[3] In addition to western Europe and northern America, other customers of British products were becoming less and less able to receive them because the prices of *their* exports (the bulk of the raw materials and foodstuffs that was imported into Britain) was declining in the world markets.[4] The British continued to buy these raw materials and foodstuffs, but with prices that were hardly enough for these areas to sustain their demand for British industrial products, let alone to expand it enough to absorb all that was produced by the technological advancement and product diversification in Britain. It seemed, then, that the British were headed toward an overproduction crisis. They attempted a variety of methods to deepen their existing markets and to extend them by incorporating new areas. At the same time, they were trying to finance the gaping deficit in their trade account. The way in which these interventions coalesced, however, compounded the incipient problems by causing a drain of bullion and capital out of Britain.[5]

Finally, the existing arrangements were further pressured by the changes in agriculture. The short harvests of 1828, 1829, and 1831 required importations of grain from Poland, Russia, and Hungary. These areas usually absorbed little of British manufactures and could not rapidly assimilate more. In any case, the landlords and rulers of these regions preferred to be paid in gold so that they could spend it on fineries from France, Italy, and Asia.[6] These periodic shortages were also the symptoms of a longer-term trend, whereby British agriculture was becoming less and less able to meet the demands of a growing population.[7] In other words, import of grains was becoming a structural rather than a seasonal necessity.[8]

In the 1830s and 1840s, Britain approached the trough of the crisis. Working people and the poor were restless because of increasing unemployment and because they did not have enough to eat. Manufacturers were despairing because they believed that the prevailing political and fiscal arrangements were inhibiting the expansionary potential of the economy.[9] The energies of the former went into the movement for the formation of a People's Charter and Parliamentary Reform; those of the merchants coalesced to support the Anti-Corn Law League and actively promoted their vision of free trade.[10]

The Corn Laws were repealed in 1846, the Navigation Laws in 1849. In 1854, foreign ships were admitted to the coastal trade of the United Kingdom, and in 1860, with the repeal of duties on 371 articles, the free-trade policy was completely in place.[11]

What was ushered in with the repeal of protectionist measures was no less than a first step in the general restructuring of not only the British, but the capitalist world economy as a whole. It was this latter development that allowed the continuation of the British hegemony for another twenty-five years under substantively new conditions.

Expansion, 1840–1876

Between the mid-1840s and the early 1870s, a growing number of new areas became participants in the changing world economic networks, the relations among the previously interrelated zones were strengthened, and Britain remained at the center of the constellation of economic and political relations that characterized the capitalist world system. Four main developments supported this expansion: (1) the gradual elimination of protectionism in much of the globe; (2) new discoveries of gold that relaxed the financial constraints of the previous decades; (3) new transportation and communication facilities which brought the distant parts of the globe closer to each other; and (4) the peace interest that came to govern the new balance of power in the interstate system. Each one of these developments stemmed independently from the social and economic circumstances of the early nineteenth century. As such they should not be regarded, individually or together, as the exogenous factors that led to the mid-Victorian boom. What was significant was that by developing more or less contemporaneously, they removed the bottlenecks that had arrested the development of the capitalist world economy, allowed for the widening and deepening of capitalist relations in the world, and strengthened the position of Britain and western Europe as the main centers of accumulation in the world economy.

Starting from the 1850s, western European and North American states responded to Britain's repeal of her protectionist measures by adopting similarly liberal trade policies. Treaties involving the lowering of tariffs were signed between the various European governments. Zollverein duties were progressively lowered toward a tariff for revenue only, levies on the important waterways of Europe were abolished, and individual governments in Europe adopted a series of measures allowing for freer trade and more secure employment of capital. These included the spread of limited liability, repeal of prohibition on usury, legalization of commercial instruments, and further improvements in commercial and company laws.[12]

Economically, the main reason that prompted the European and American states to respond to British overtures for freer trade derived from Britain's inordinate share of world trade and the potential for further expansion under a more permissive framework.[13] In the newly incorporated and peripheral zones, free movement of goods and capital was secured through the use of political pressures and sometimes through military force. It was through such interventions that Britain obtained the signing of Treaties of "Free Trade and Friendship" with the Ottoman and Persian Empires, and opened the Chinese markets for opium imports in 1839–42.[14]

World gold production increased in leaps and bounds, especially between the late 1840s and the early 1870s, removing one of the most confining bottlenecks in the world economy.[15] Most of the newly discovered gold was drawn into the core areas of the capitalist world economy through the operation of "a swarm of gold mining companies and merchant houses that buzzed around the stock exchange in 1852 and 1853,"[16] as well as by way of direct exports.[17] As the reserves of the main banks were replenished and continued to rise,[18] the issue and the supply of paper money increased,[19] eventually leading to a reversal of the downward trend of European prices.[20]

Generation of new liquidity reinvigorated the economic activities in western Europe and, by extension, in the rest of the world economy. A major part of capital that was exported from Britain after the 1850s was invested in railways and public utilities. Some of it was exported as public or private loans to augment the purchasing capacity of the receiving zones, thereby providing further relief from the possible glutting of the British markets.[21]

Over 100,000 miles of new rail line were laid in the world between 1850 and 1870, as opposed to 23,000 in all the years before.[22] More than 90% of these new lines were concentrated in Europe and North America.[23] It is no exaggeration to say that construction of railroads and the spreading use of the electric telegraph were among the most remarkable achievements of the third quarter of the nineteenth century. By bringing distant markets closer, by connecting the sources of raw materials with centers of production, and, through backward linkages, by contributing to metallurgical industries and coal production, railroads helped deepen capitalist relations, especially in the core areas of the capitalist world economy between the 1840s and 1870s.[24] The expansion of rail networks in England, Europe, and the world also undermined the pivotal position of the old entrepôts and, finally, served as a powerful vehicle for the centralization of capital under the purview of big financial institutions.[25]

Communication of messages by telegraph was another important achievement of this period. Between 1848 and 1860, almost all of Europe and North America became parts of a network whereby two thousand words could be sent in one hour between any two places.[26] With the laying of submarine cables across the Atlantic, the scope of and the rapidity with which information could be collected and disseminated in the world economy reached unprecedented levels. Along with railroads, the telegraph also transformed warfare, expanded methods of domestic surveillance, and improved the general efficiency of administration by states within the world system.

Compared with the scope of hostilities at the turn of the nineteenth and the twentieth centuries, the wars of the nineteenth century stand out with their brevity and their localized nature. On the basis of the absence of a general war, we can characterize the one hundred years between 1815 and 1914 as relatively peaceful.[27] But the configuration of forces that limited warfare in Europe did not remain the same throughout this period.

Generally, the western European settlement in the aftermath of the Napoleonic Wars was beneficial to Britain. The war had ended not only with the defeat of Britain's most powerful rival, France, but the Spanish and the Portuguese links with South America were severed as well.[28] Political boundaries in Europe were rationalized, allowing Britain to maintain a protective hand over the sea and river ports of commercial importance.[29] Eastern Europe, on the other hand, was left to be policed by the Holy Alliance, which was formed by the coalition of the Russian, Austrian, and the Prussian aristocracies, with the sanctification of the church, and under the leadership of the tsar. The primary interest of these monarchs was in holding their multi-ethnic empires together by suppressing the secessionist agitation of their subject people.[30]

Significant changes occurred in this configuration after the 1840s. These can be traced to two developments. First, as the economic difficulties of the first half of the nineteenth century became more serious, different classes of people exerted pressure on their governments for a more equitable distribution of the rewards of capitalist production.[31] Most western European states were able to find ways of appeasing these demands and ensuring a medium to long-term tranquility within their national borders, and hence imprinting their status within the interstate system with relative strength and stability.[32] The empires of eastern Europe, on the other hand, were saddled with nationalism, which as a political movement grew out of the upheavals of the first half of the nineteenth century and eventually became one of the most important forces that undermined the structure of these empires.

The second development that affected interstate politics in about 1840 stemmed from the conflicting visions held by Britain (as the hegemonic power in the capitalist world economy) and Russia (the strongest of the empires in Europe). Russia perceived its future in southward expansion. This could hamper British access to India and constitute a major obstacle in the way of the unification of the world economy under British hegemony. Toward the late 1830s, as Britain was expanding its sphere of influence, Russia strengthened its position within the Holy Alliance and gained an unexpected but very valuable access to the sultan's court by signing the Treaty of Hünkâr İskelesi in 1833. From that point onward, Britain and Russia were on a collision course and they finally clashed in Crimea. The Crimean War was the only conflagration in which more than two European powers directly participated during the nineteenth century. It was fought under the leadership of Britain, over the territories of the Ottoman Empire, with the primary purpose of containing Russia. Its conclusion was important in that the unequivocal defeat of the Russians helped deflect the tendency toward a general war in Europe for another six decades.[33]

Following the war, the relative strengths of the European states were such that the interstate system allowed for many different combinations among them, leading to a kaleidoscope of successive alliances and hence to a more stable and longer-term peace in Europe.[34] Furthermore, this configuration of forces, which is commonly referred to as the "concert of Europe," embodied the interests of a new social stratum of grand bourgeoisie—that is, of bankers, merchants, and big industrialists—in broadening the scope of their operations preferably in a peaceful environment.[35]

Results

Removal of mercantilist barriers, discoveries of gold, development of transportation and communication networks, and the absence of a general war in Europe created favorable conditions for the circulation of goods, people, and capital in the world economy in the second half of the nineteenth century. For example, between 1800 and 1830 world trade had increased by 30%, from about 300 million to about 400 million pounds; but between 1840 and 1870, it multiplied five times over; and by 1870, it passed 2,800 million pounds. The annual rate growth of total European exports was 2.9% in early 1840, and 6.0% in the early 1870s.[36] Again by 1870, the volume of foreign trade for every citizen of the United Kingdom, France, Germany, Austria, and Scandinavia was between four and five times what it had been in 1830. Between 1800 and 1840, about one million Europeans had migrated to the United States, but between 1840 and 1870, seven million crossed the Atlantic. By the early 1840s, Britain had accumulated about 160 million pounds in credits abroad; but between 1855 and 1870, the British invested at the rate of 29 million a year, and by 1873 their accumulated balances had almost reached 1,000 million pounds.[37]

Strengthening of the ligaments of the world economy in these years was accomplished on a laterally expanding basis with the incorporation of new areas into the networks of its operation, and it was intertwined with the development of a new global division of labor. Under this new alignment of economic zones, agricultural and raw material production shifted from England and certain parts of Europe towards the "European periphery," North America, and subsequently to Africa.[38] Owing to historical, geographical, and political conditions, certain parts of western Europe (specifically, the northeast corner of France, Belgium, and Westphalia)[39] and England were in a good position to readjust their economic priorities and concentrate their resources in the more profitable ventures of the epoch, such as the exploration and exploitation of new coal beds and iron ores, steel and textile mills, and (later in the century) electric and chemical industries.[40] In the mid-nineteenth century, by referring to this pattern of specialization, we can clearly distinguish between two economic zones in the world economy. One was where the newer and most profitable (mostly industrial) production was located and financial operations were centered. England was the hub of this part. It was the leading producer of industrial goods, the largest trader, and its currency the most important medium of exchange in the world.[41] Industrial and financial growth followed diverse trajectories in other parts of Europe,[42] but in the end Britain and western Europe came to account for close to four-fifths of the world's output of manufactures.[43]

In the other extreme were the areas that increasingly became specialized in the cultivation of those cash crops and agricultural and raw materials that were displaced from western Europe. It was from these places that western Europe was beginning to draw most of its needs. While there would be little, if any, disagreement in characterizing the entire first zone as "central" or "core," the status of the second could be determined only by dividing it into two subzones. First were the settler societies: the United States, Canada, Australia, and New Zealand. The geography, climate, and natural endowments of these places gave them certain advantages over others. Also, the exclusive form of settlement that took place in them brought with it the possibility of acquiring a political leverage vis-à-vis the core states.[44] Settlers were ultimately successful in combining these elements and using them to compete with and displace the older centers of production from the world market in grains and animal fibres. The most important of these products were wheat in midwestern United States, Canada, and Australia, and mutton and wool in Australia and New Zealand.[45] Subsequently, these areas diversified their economic activities and achieved a production mix that enabled them to attain a semiperipheral position in the world economy. Two nonsettler societies, namely, the Austrian and the Russian empires, would also be included in this group, even though they had been politically weakened as a result of their incorporation into the world economy: Austria, because it became the primary overland intermediary for East-West trade; and Russia, because its land mass was left intact during and after its incorporation, which made utilizing the advantages of size possible.

Most of the other areas that were not subjected to exclusive settlement, specialized in the production of some raw material or foodstuff: nitrates and copper in Chile, guano in Peru, cotton in Egypt, vegetable oils in Africa are examples of this category.[46] Formal colonization, informal control, market forces, the structural position of a European minority who chose to settle in some of these places, or the interests of some domestic classes, were instrumental in helping to establish such activities in these places. Particular forms of labor control that were utilized here made them intermittently competitive in the crops of their specialization. They expanded the volume of their production and exports in tandem with the growing demand from the core areas. But social conditions and the relations of domination that existed between them and the core areas prevented these zones from fully exploiting their competitive advantages or from diversifying into more remunerative activities. Consequently, in most instances, the real beneficiaries of their export surpluses were the European financiers, capitalists and their intermediaries who had organized the trade and production networks.[47] By and large, the peripheral zone of the capitalist world economy in the mid-nineteenth century was composed of areas that exhibited some combination of these social and historical properties. Within Europe, too, there had developed a peripheral belt extending from Ireland through Andulusia, southern France and Sicily to the Balkans, encircling the northwestern corner of the continent. Sulphur in Sicily and wine in southern France and Portugal were examples of monoculture activity in this peripheral region.[48] Competitive disadvantages (mainly, land exhaustion, overpopulation, distance from the main arteries of transportation), and their historical relationship to the other parts of Europe were among the factors that separated them from the trajectory of the rest of Europe.[49] Also, in some instances, both in Europe and elsewhere, political movements were premised upon tapping the peripheral status of a particular region. However unequal they might have been, intensification of exchange relations within the world economy generated some returns for some groups who were controlling the local extensions of these relations and who could augment these benefits by establishing political control over that area. Romanian independence as well as the position of the southern states during the American Civil War constitute examples of such projects.[50]

The Place of the Ottoman Empire

Long-term evaluation of the economic and political variables indicate that during the first three quarters of the nineteenth century the links between the Ottoman Empire and the capitalist world economy became closer and that the content of these relations were such that the position of the Ottoman Empire within the world political and economic networks was resembling that of the peripheral areas of that system. To give a few examples, during the first three quarters of the nineteenth century, Ottoman foreign trade increased fourfold; this was accompanied by a capital inflow from the core that, starting from a negligible amount at the turn of the nineteenth century, had surpassed thirty million pounds by the early 1870s.[51] Also during these years, the processes that had been implanted through incorporation culminated in the decisive shift of the orientation of the Ottoman foreign trade networks from the Near East and Asia toward western Europe and the United States. Following the withdrawal of French maritime power from the eastern Mediterranean, Britain became the major trade partner of the Ottoman Empire and also supplied most of the capital that was invested there. In the early 1870s, over 27% of Ottoman exports were destined for Britain (representing a twofold increase from 13.3% in 1830–32) and over 30% of Ottoman imports originated from Britain (up from 19% in 1830–32).[52] In exchange for cotton and woolen textiles, agricultural and other machinery, iron, coal, and kerosene that made up most of its imports, the Ottoman Empire was exporting some of the typical peripheral goods of the era such as cereals, cotton, natural dyestuffs, silk, opium, various fruits, and nuts. Over 90% of the capital that flowed into the empire did so as government loans, and the remainder was invested in railroads, public utilities, and other infrastructure that supported the commercial links. Also during the middle decades of the nineteenth century, the participation of the Ottoman Empire within the interstate system was formalized with the signing of the Paris Peace Treaty at the end of the Crimean War.[53]

A closer examination of the long-term growth and intensification of the economic and political relations between the Ottoman Empire and the capitalist world economy in the nineteenth century reveals that they proceeded through three distinct phases, separated by two turning points. The years between the end of the Napoleonic Wars and the 1840s were marked by the faster growth of Ottoman imports than its exports and with little, if any, foreign investment.[54] It was also in this period that Britain increased its share in Ottoman foreign trade by about 400%.[55] In other words, the eastern Mediterranean, including Ottoman territories, became a customer of British commodities during these years.[56] Two factors helped propel these areas into such a status. First was the Ottoman difficulties of obtaining manufactured goods from the customary sources in France and Austria.[57] The second was the unrestrictive import policy of the Ottoman Empire, which was further liberalized with the signing of the Free Trade treaties in 1838.[58] Armed with these measures and with the removal of the restrictive monopolies of the Levant Company,[59] the British, after a series of false starts, finally managed to displace Indian textiles from the Ottoman markets after the 1830s.[60]

After the mid-nineteenth century, the British began to augment their imports from the Ottoman Empire. In tandem with their pursuits in other parts of the periphery (especially Latin America), they hoped that the expansion of Ottoman exports would enable the Ottomans to purchase more British products. Direct payments to the Ottoman Empire in the form of loans and capital exports was a crucial component of this policy. A part of these funds was used by the Porte to finance the deficit in the trade account of the empire; another part to finance the infrastructure that was related to trade; and a third part was directly invested by the British in Ottoman export-oriented agriculture. Such material support combined with favorable conditions in world markets seemed to bear fruit; during the mid-Victorian years there was an unprecedented expansion in Ottoman exports. Not only was the rate of export growth generally higher than imports during these years, but in a rare development for the empire, the value of exports actually surpassed imports, in 1851, 1852, and 1862.[61]

Alternating relations of hegemony and rivalry that characterized the different phases of the development of the capitalist world system in the nineteenth century also had important effects on the position of the Ottoman Empire within that system. The global hegemony of Britain corresponded to the period when this state became the major economic partner of the empire and, diplomatically, the most influential foreign power at the Porte. It was also in this period that Britain sponsored the admission of the Ottoman state to the concert of Europe and persuaded other European powers to participate in the pledge she had already made regarding the territorial integrity of the Ottoman Empire.[62]

With the reversal of the world market trends in the late nineteenth century, imports reappeared as the main economic activity linking the empire with European markets. In addition to continuing to absorb the products of European industries, the Ottoman Empire was also drawn into the ambit of supranational capital, which had become the main organizational grid of the capitalist world economy during the last quarter of the nineteenth century.[63]

In each of the periods delineated above, we find the Ottoman Empire as engaging in a series of economic activities that were geared toward providing relief from various conjunctural problems of the world economy.[64] This assessment suggests that between 1800 and 1876 the Ottoman Empire was, in fact, gradually pushed to the periphery of the world system from what had promised to be a more intermediate position at the end of incorporation.

To analyze how this came about, we turn to the political context within which these changes were taking place. Here, the key factor was the substantive weakness of the Ottoman state. The incorporation of the Ottoman Empire had undercut the political strength of the Ottoman bureaucracy. The British policy in the Near East contributed to the weakness of the Ottoman state because its two aims—namely, the protection of the Ottoman state and the promotion of free trade—were in conflict with each other. And finally, there were the growing divisions within the bureaucracy which rendered most of the state policies ineffective or incoherent in the long run.

THE STATE, 1815-1876

The Ottoman Bureaucracy and Incorporation

The integration of the Ottoman Empire into the capitalist world economy unleashed processes that endangered the territorial integrity of the empire, undermined the political sovereignty of her rulers, and threw doubt upon the long-term existence of the Ottoman government itself. In terms of their manifestations and their effects on the imperial center, these processes can be classified into two groups. Under the first one fall the military campaigns that were staged by different European powers and the secessionist movements that engulfed various subject groups and set them against the Ottoman center. These were the formal threats against the Ottoman Empire. The second one comprises the reorganization of the social and economic networks in various localities that linked them directly to the core areas of the capitalist world economy by circumventing the imperial apparatus, particularly the treasury. Elements of substantive decentralization were rooted in this domain.

Through military reform, diplomatic efforts, and suppressing or coopting the centrifugal tendencies, the bureaucrats were fairly successful in stabilizing the formal challenges to their rule during the first half of the nineteenth century. They limited their territorial losses and maintained a semblance of formal control even over those areas that were only tenuously linked to the imperial center, such as Moldavia, Wallachia, and Egypt. The negative effect of the most threatening of the revolts, such as those of the Serbians and the Greeks, were likewise kept to a minimum. Most significantly, by the end of the first decades of the nineteenth century, the Ottomans had already acquired the means of channeling all of their interstate problems to the court of the European Concert. The increased premium that was placed on the solution of conflicts through peaceful methods of negotiations and treaties gave the Ottomans a breathing space. After the incessant wars and rebellions of the late eighteenth and early nineteenth centuries, the empire lived through two long stretches of relative calm; one extending from the Crimean War to the Ottoman-Russian War of 1877; and the other from 1878 to the Balkan Wars of 1911–12. These conditions allowed the bureaucrats to address the problems, which were rooted in the substantive decentralization of the empire.

Tanzimat: A Bureaucratic Response to Substantive Decentralization

After they managed to contain the formal challenges to their sovereignty, the bureaucrats attempted to reestablish their claim over the existing taxes and also to create new revenue sources for the central government. They tried to achieve this primarily through an institutional restructuring of the imperial apparatus and by formulating a series of policies within the newly created framework, culminating in a broad program of reorganization, known as *Tanzimat* in Ottoman historiography. The main thrust of these measures was to simplify the collection of revenues. Accordingly, steps were taken to centralize the treasury, and to delegate the responsibility of tax collection to the salaried agents of the government (*muhassıls*), rather than governors, holders of prebendal grants, or other intermediaries of the classical system.[65] A uniform tithe was set in the entire empire, thereby ending the classical pattern, where the rates had varied widely in different provinces.[66] Market dues and urban taxes were combined into a single profit tax (*temettü vergisi*), and the poll tax that had been levied on non-Muslim communities was changed into a military exemption tax. In an effort to strengthen central control, local administrators and judges were prohibited from collecting dues, fees, and surtaxes that did not have legal foundation. This was a significant departure from the older practice, where such collection had constituted the main income of these functionaries.

In essence, these measures amounted to a move toward direct taxation in cash. To support this and to accommodate the ongoing monetization of the Ottoman economy in general, the government took steps to completely overhaul the currency system. A new 5 kuruş (*beşlik*) and a new 6 kuruş (*altılık*) coins were minted in 1829 and 1833, respectively. In 1839, hand-written bonds of 25 kuruş value carrying 12% interest were issued to take the place of paper money, which had been absent from the Ottoman Empire until then.[67] In the 1840s, the government tried for the first time to coordinate internal and external values of various Ottoman coins by adopting a fixed bimetallic (i.e., gold and silver) standard. Following a series of adjustments between 1844 and 1847, the ratio of 1:15.909 was set in 1847.[68] In the same year, a new gold coin (*mecidiye*) was struck at the nominal value of 100 kuruş and the exchange rate of the Ottoman kuruş was fixed at 110 kuruş = 1 pound sterling. The Porte sponsored the establishment of a bank in Istanbul whose responsibility was to maintain this exchange rate by entering into appropriate transactions in Europe.[69] To control and regulate credit transactions, the government also fixed the rate of interest on short-term loans at 8% per annum in 1848, and raised it to 12% in 1852. Credit needs of different sectors and regions were assessed through provincial surveys and an Agricultural Credit Fund was established to provide loans to farmers.[70] Finally, all of these reorganizations and policies were placed under the purview of the newly established Ministry of Finance, which, in 1860–61, had also undertaken the responsibility for drafting the first ever state budget in the Ottoman Empire.[71]

Paralleling these interventions were a series of initiatives that were designed to win back the loyalty of the influential merchants and notables in various localities. For example, non-Muslim and Muslim merchants who were involved in foreign and transit trade of the empire were organized into separate corporate bodies as *Avrupa* and *Hayriye Tüccarları*, respectively, and consuls (*şehbender*) were appointed to represent them.[72] Under these arrangements, by offering special inducements, the central government was trying to lure the non-Muslim merchants away from seeking foreign protection.

In a similar vein, the bureaucracy tried to draw the local notables into the formal hierarchy of Ottoman administration by granting them official titles, not only as ayans but also as governors and mütesellims.[73] Newly formed provincial councils constituted an additional vehicle through which the ayan acquired responsibility and official authority over the administration of their localities.[74] At the same time, the government attempted to limit the independent influence of the ayan by carrying out cadastral surveys (in 1838 and 1856), and by enacting the Provincial Law of 1864. The surveys aimed at assessing and registering the conditions and especially the tax liability of landed property in the provinces.[75] The Provincial Law redefined and redrew the administrative divisions and spheres of responsibilities for local officials in a way that cut into the power of both the governors and the ayan.[76]

Finally, mention should be made of the reorganization of judicial structures and processes whereby all the previous initiatives were made parts of a new legal order.[77] A penal code was drafted in 1840 (and amended in 1851); a land law, in 1858; and a Law of Transactions (*Mecelle*), between 1869–76. Particularly important was the Land Law of 1858, which gave de facto recognition to small peasant proprietorship while including explicit restrictions on the expansion of the size of such holdings.[78] In 1867, in a major concession, the Porte granted foreigners the right to own immovable property in the Ottoman Empire. Through the establishment of consular and mixed courts, and adjustments in the acceptability of the testimony of non-Muslims, the procedures of adjudicating cases between Muslims and non-Muslims were based on universally recognized principles. Also, in an effort to secure the allegiance of non-Muslim groups to the Ottoman government, the central bureaucracy passed a Nationality Act and a Law of Passports, while at the same time the Jewish, Armenian, and Greek communities were permitted to draw up their own separate constitutions.[79]

In intent, if not in practice, these policies amounted to a comprehensive program addressing most (if not all) of the problems that were undermining the social and territorial integrity of the empire. Furthermore, formal and substantive strengthening, which would have resulted from them, did not necessarily threaten the general interests and objectives of the dominant powers of the capitalist world economy. After all, a better administered empire would make a more viable buffer against the Russians, and better promote Ottoman territories both as reliable markets for the British commodities and as a haven for foreign capital.[80] Beyond the general objective of arresting the disintegration of the empire, no pronounced tendency toward protectionism or mercantilism prevailed among the policymakers of the Tanzimat era.[81] On the contrary, they willingly adopted measures of economic liberalization, especially when these were likely to improve their chances of receiving political protection from the European states. Willingness of the Ottoman bureaucracy to cooperate with the European powers also made it easy for the British government to generate domestic support for its policy of backing the Ottoman government.[82]

Given all this, it is not surprising that the Tanzimat policies were met with enthusiastic support in Europe, so much so that some of the subsequent analyses have ignored the local pressures that originally shaped these policies, and have interpreted them as aspects of westernization that was materially and/or ideologically inspired by Europe.

Ultimately, however, the success of Tanzimat depended not on its scope or the kind of support it attracted from Europe but on the generation of a sound financial basis. From the outset, the bureaucrats were keenly aware of this requirement. They perceived fiscal solvency as a key to long-term territorial and administrative integrity of the empire, and they were adamant about instituting their reforms in this and other fields without having to resort to European markets for loans. So strong was their fear of the political compromise that could result from indebtedness that even after all of their initial attempts failed to restore and expand the revenue base of the government, they continued to resist the idea of borrowing from abroad. In 1850 and 1852, when the Grand Viziers Reshid and Ali Pashas signed agreements with Europeans for loans of fifty million and fifty-five million francs, respectively, the Porte refused ratification, and the Sultan dismissed the Viziers despite the fact that these cancellations cost the government considerable sums in indemnity.[83] In the course of the discussions regarding the second loan, one of the advisers to the sultan specifically cited the dispatch of a British fleet to Piraeus as a result of the failure of the Greeks to pay their debts as grounds for not going along with the agreement.[84] But in the end, the expenses of the Crimean War proved to be too heavy for the Porte to meet with domestic resouces, and in 1856, the Ottoman government floated its first loan in the European markets.[85]

As had been feared by the bureaucrats, this and the subsequent loans opened up formal channels through which the foreign creditors obtained ways of directly influencing the administration of the government. Shortly after the issuing of the first loan, the Ottoman Imperial Bank was established, predominantly with foreign capital.[86] The British were quick in claiming and acquiring substantial control over the operations of this bank. In 1856, the Austrian government dispatched a financial adviser to the Porte. Two years later, British and French delegates joined him to form the High Council of the Treasury. In 1860, this council was expanded and transformed into *Conseil Supèrieur des Finances* and rose to prominence as the principal supervisor of the financial reforms in the Ottoman Empire. The government also yielded to foreign pressure and agreed to having representatives of foreign holders of Ottoman bonds on the Conseil. After the 1860s, this institution acquired direct control over the administration of state revenues that were earmarked for serving the growing debt of the government.[87] Between the 1850s and the 1870s, the external liabilities of the Ottoman state multiplied quickly, and finally, in 1876, the Porte had to make a formal declaration of its insolvency. The Public Debt Administration, which was set up to replace the Conseil in 1881, immediately acquired a permanent position in the fiscal administration of the empire.

Had the unfolding of history been different, that is, had the bureaucrats been successful in providing the Ottoman Empire with the much-desired financial security, this, combined with the support that foreign governments were willing to extend, could have helped chart the course of social change in the Ottoman Empire toward *semi*peripheralization. Without such a financial fulcrum, however, the Ottoman Empire had no basis for rebounding. Consequently, diplomatic support and reform measures that were supposed to serve as the substantive braces of a stronger state ended up as threads that wove a thick crust around a decrepit structure, which, in the end, had to be propped up from within by an institution that was closely affiliated with supranational finance capital. The failure of the Ottoman bureaucracy in this respect can be attributed to two main factors. The first was the growing incompatibility among the different aims of the British policies in regard to the Ottoman Empire. The second factor grew out of the divisions within the bureaucratic class, and from the incongruity between the substantively new circumstances that surrounded the Ottoman state and the relatively old means with which the central bureaucracy tried to implement its reforms.

Reasons for Failure

British Policy in the Near East. In their approach to the Ottoman Empire during the nineteenth century, the British were motivated by two kinds of interests. The first of these was the political aim of sustaining the territorial integrity of the empire as both a buffer against Russian belligerence and a safe passage to Asia. The second was more economic in nature. Here, the British were concerned with promoting the free movement of Ottoman goods in and around the Ottoman Empire and supporting the development of Ottoman territories as a dependable outlet for British commodities. While in principle the British and the Ottoman governments were in harmony in both of these aims, in practice the particulars of one group of policies often contradicted and undermined the other. Especially in the absence of the financial underpinnings that were so essential for the simultaneous pursuit of political and economic ends, the tendency toward liberalization of trade prevailed over the competing end of sustaining the Ottoman state.

The problems that arose in implementing the provisions of the free trade treaties in the late 1830s constitute a good example of how the two ends of the joint Anglo- (and also Euro-) Ottoman policy became incompatible with each other. The Ottoman government signed the first such treaty with Britain in 1838. This and the following treaties that were signed with France (1838), Hanseatic towns, the United States, Sardinia (1839); Sweden and Norway, the Netherlands, Prussia, Belgium (1840); Denmark, Toscana (1841) made Ottoman trade "one of the most liberal in the world."[88]

The regulatory aspects of these arrangements did not pose a direct or immediate threat to the Ottoman state.[89] It is true that the duty on exports was set to be higher than that on the imports (12% as opposed to 5%) but this could be seen as a continuation of the classical policy of encouraging imports over exports. In fact, with these treaties the duty on imports was *raised* from 3% to 5%, which meant that the Ottoman government stood to gain from the projected expansion in foreign trade. As for internal duties, most of these had been imposed in the first place, by local potentates who had taken advantage of the weakness of the central bureaucracy in the late eighteenth century. Thus, the limits placed on them were likely to undermine the position of local officials and provincial notables more than they would the central government.[90]

The immediate purpose of the free trade treaties, that is linking Ottoman trade to a series of principles, did not contradict the bureaucratic aim of overseeing and deriving revenue from Ottoman involvement in global economic networks. On the contrary, these treaties were premised upon the multilateral recognition of the right of the Ottoman state to tax its foreign trade as the only legitimate authority to do so.

Nevertheless, the consequences of these liberal principles turned out to be more significant in terms of the effective limits they placed on the ability of the Ottoman state to supervise and benefit from this trade than in enhancing the position of the government. For example, the abolition of the monopolies took effect immediately. As a result, the government had to relinquish a considerable source of revenue,[91] and it was effectively barred from controlling the movement of goods in and around the empire. But the expansion of the Ottoman foreign trade that was supposed to generate revenue for the Ottoman government lagged behind. When it took place, this expansion was propelled by forces that were independent of both government policies of promotion and of the provisions of these treaties.[92] Furthermore, in spite of the original intention of both the Ottoman and British governments to restrict the applicability of these agreements to foreign trade, the meaning of their stipulations were stretched, and soon British subjects and Ottomans who were protected by the British Embassy claimed "the right to open shops as tailors and shoemakers even though these trades in [İstanbul] were incorporated [under the auspices of the government] and no Turk not a member of the corporation [could] exercise them."[93] Also, while foreign products were free to move within the empire after the payment of 5% duty, local products that were being transported from one locality to another by Muslim merchants were still subject to various extra duties.[94]

Finally, free trade treaties of the 1830s had the indirect effect of weakening the domestic legitimacy of the bureaucratic overrule. The regulations that were brought by their stipulations, and the reform measures that accompanied them, created the impression that the Ottoman government, in alliance with foreign states, was becoming unduly protective of its non-Muslim subjects.

Divided Bureaucracy: The Imperial Janus. The second major factor that rendered Tanzimat policies inherently weak and ineffective stemmed from within the bureaucratic apparatus itself. Here, there were two kinds of problems. One of them concerned the divisions within the bureaucracy; the other, the way in which this ruling elite related to the societal processes that had engulfed the Ottoman Empire.

By the first years of the nineteenth century, the separate existence of the Ottoman government (i.e., the Sublime Porte) as distinct from the Palace (or the person of the sultan) had become well entrenched.[95] The military had all but lost the privileged position it had held and was replaced by the Foreign Office as the pinnacle of the administrative hierarchy. Both the Foreign and the Prime Minister's offices came to be staffed by a handful of bureaucrats who rose from the Translation Office with backgrounds and education that differed substantially from that of the classical servants of the sultan.

There is no reason to doubt that for the most part, these Tanzimat officials were committed to reforming the empire. They were unequivocal in their belief that the rightful place of the Ottoman Empire was with the great powers of Europe and that strengthening the empire was indispensable for realizing that goal. Alongside of this group, however, there were still a large number of officials who had been trained by and for the old war machine. The apparent intimacy between the European embassies and the reforming bureaucrats as well as the lifestyles and backgrounds of the new elite provoked the resentment and hostility of this older group. These "conservatives" circulated in and out of higher echelons of the bureaucratic hierarchy to dilute, discontinue or even reverse some of the reform measures. Later on, the growing influence of the European governments on the day-to-day administration of the empire generated a further response which, in its long-term effects, was more significant than the narrower infighting at the highest levels. Starting from the 1860s, some of the junior bureaucrats who occupied marginal positions in the central government organized an opposition movement under the banner of New Ottomanism. They proposed a synthesis between Islam and selected elements from European societies as a solution to the problems of the empire.[96]

Underlying the divisions within the ruling class of the Ottoman Empire was the continuing shrinkage of the revenues that could be collected from the subjects and used to staff and run the proliferating state apparatus. Consequently, those who were holding office tried to protect their position and improve their income at all costs by resorting to bribery, corruption, and defamation of their rivals. According to the contemporary chronicler Lütfi, the great preoccupations of those times were three: to drive out one's rivals; to bring in one's friends; to silence the tongues of the people paying close attention to the price of bread and other necessities.[97]

However deep and debilitating these divisions might have been, all sections of the bureaucracy, including the old, new, and the rebellious groups, were strikingly similar in their approach to rule-making. They all started from the premise that the imperial structures could be reorganized (or conserved) through an array of rules, regulations, and legislations that were articulated, drafted, and issued by a closely knit group of officials in Istanbul.[98] Even the New Ottomans, who tried hard to broaden their appeal, failed to break the image of a narrow group of bureaucrats who were debating among themselves about "how to save the Empire." The image of a strong empire that inspired and motivated the bureaucratic class was rooted, above all, in the classical *weltanschauung*. This is apparent not only in their approach to rule-making, but also in the content and result of some of the measures they tried to implement during the nineteenth century.[99]

Also, the assumption that the classical power relations were still intact put the Ottoman government in the untenable position of having to rely on the remnants of the old administrative hierarchy for implementing reforms and for collecting the old and new taxes.[100] In practice, this created a situation where each of the reform ordinances were distilled through the successive layers of public authority and were refracted by various groups who had interposed themselves between Istanbul and the loci of production, trade, and provincial administration. Often, by the time they reached their site of actual implementation, governmental policies had been reinterpreted so many times that they had little chance of generating the originally intended results. In provincial administration, continuing shrinkage of already inadequate resources led to an acri-monious struggle for survival. The governors especially, whose means of augmenting their fixed income were curtailed and whose traditional rights to locally collected taxes were revoked, were trying to supplement their salaries by using all the means they had access to. In addition to finding ways of imposing surtaxes and illegal dues, the governors now had to cultivate alliances with some of the competing loci of power at the center not only to ensure the provisioning of their households but also to protect their tenure. In this respect, the governor of Diyarbekir was very forthcoming in expressing the predicament that the local administrators were in during the late 1850s: "I have no inducement to be honest. If I attempt to rule justly, all of the other pashas will combine against me and I shall soon be turned out of my place and unless I take bribes I shall be too poor to purchase another."[101] Needless to say, with all these constraints and insecurity, neither the governors nor any of the other links in the administrative chain were in a position to bear the burden of a long-term commitment to reorganizing the state apparatus that the reform measures were demanding of them.

The problem was, the transformation of the social structures in the Ottoman Empire had gone too far to be reversed, harnessed, or coopted by a single stroke of a comprehensive land code or that of the provincial law or by the promises contained therein. Most important, the Ottoman imperial apparatus had ceased to be the exclusive source of power in Ottoman society. A number of groups had widened their influence during the incorporation of the Ottoman Empire into the capitalist world economy. Among these, local notables, tax farmers, merchants and money-lenders were the most important. The last group especially had come to control a wide network of informal credit that covered all tax farming transactions and most of the trade that took place in the empire. Even the treasury and the leading bureaucrats had accu-mulated large debts to these private bankers who were the only de-pendable source of liquid funds in the empire prior to the government's acceptance of foreign loans. The bureaucrats' response to the growing power of the ayan was to incorporate them into the administrative structure by delegating official responsibilities. Granting new rights to non-Muslims, which was a part of the judicial reforms, was used for similar purposes. Through these interventions the bureaucracy was trying to mold the new heterogeneity into a monolithic Ottomanism. The problem was, however, that these groups were not interested in aiding the government in its quest for reestablishing the classical centrality of the empire. For it was precisely disorder and anarchy that had allowed local merchants, money-lenders and the provincial potentates the op-portunity to accumulate wealth and rise to prominence. The notions of equality and justice that the Tanzimat bureaucrats espoused were far from addressing the real concerns of the non-Muslim strata. After all with all the privileges of extraterritorial protection they had acquired and the economic opportunities they had profitably exploited, these people were neither equal and homogeneous nor were they interested in being recognized as such before the Ottoman courts.

There are three developments that took place in the mid-nineteenth century which stand out as exceptions (if not historical alternatives) to classical patrimonialism, which otherwise proved to be the all-pervasive force that shaped the general thrust of the Tanzimat policies. These are, first, the special commission that was summoned to Istanbul in 1845 to discuss the needs of the provinces; second, the provincial councils that were expanded in membership and authority as part of the Provincial Law of 1864; and third, the constitutionalist movement to which a section of the New Ottomans joined. This culminated in the proclamation of the first Ottoman constitution in 1876, the election and convening of a Chamber of Deputies in 1877. What distinguishes these developments from the other Tanzimat policies and institutions is that their participants, at least in part, came from among people who had already acquired power and respect of their communities privately, that is, without benefiting from the amenities of official posts. As such, they contained (at least potentially) elements of an alternative approach to reorganizing the Ottoman imperial structures. Especially, the Con-stitution of 1876 and the Chamber of Deputies that followed its pro-clamation can be seen as the crystallization of a discourse of opposition that was initially articulated by the New Ottomans. This was especially manifest in the composition of the assembly and the independence the chamber exhibited in its deliberations and decisions during the one year it was in session.[102]

Nevertheless, the general indecisiveness on the governmental level permeated these bodies and movements as well. The Aydın delegates of the 1845 commission included the chief clerk of the Custom House, an ex-governor, and primates, along with private merchants and property owners.[103] Moreover, most of these representatives were "extremely puzzled" and "humbled" for having been consulted about the future direction of the empire. Whatever suggestions they finally made were not taken seriously.[104] As for the provincial councils, these were pre-dominantly staffed by local notables. But by the nineteenth century, these groups could no longer be regarded as true representatives of their regions, since the fealty of the populace to these ayan had long become dubious at best.[105] As for the Constitution and the Chamber of Deputies, these failed to bring a clear formula for a power-sharing arrangement between the elected deputies, the Porte, and the Palace. As a result, they were easily manipulated by Sultan Abdülhamid, who used the brief period of constitutional monarchy to undermine the power of the reforming bureaucrats. Then, by taking advantage of the loopholes in the Constitution, he closed the assembly and once again forced a shift in the locus of power from the Porte to the Palace.[106]

The third, and in some ways the most curcial, factor that underlay both the failure of these policies and the ongoing peripheral integration was rooted in the changing social structures of the Ottoman Empire.

THE SOCIETY

If the British and the Ottoman officials could find a way of linking up with the changing social structures then they could hope to succeed in reversing the substantive decentralization of the empire. The new social reality that confronted them had developed outside the purview of both the Ottoman and the British government. Tax farmers, merchants, and, above all, money-lenders who had captured the pivotal points of the new economic networks, had acquired wealth and influence independently of both of these entities. By the mid-nineteenth century, their power had equaled, and in some ways surpassed, that of the bureaucratic elite. Furthermore, due to the manner in which the Ottoman Empire had been incorporated into the world economy, these societal transformations occurred in a regionally diverse and temporally incongruous pattern. The Ottoman bureaucracy had little to offer to the dominant groups of these new networks in return for their cooperation. *Ceteris paribus,* the regulation that the government was trying to impose was anathema to the tax farmers, merchants, and the money-lenders who had prospered in an environment of economic anarchy. Their preference for a weak state and for the continuation of relations with the world economy in a manner that was devoid of organizational and structural stability distinguished these groups as a peripheral bourgeoisie from their counterparts in the core and the semiperipheral areas, who had come to exert more direct influence on their state apparati. These societal configurations which underlay the peripheralization of the Ottoman Empire can best be depicted from a local perspective. The classical and the lengthy commercial importance of western Anatolia makes this a suitable site for this purpose.

Western Anatolia: Some General Observations

In the eighteenth century, about one-third of French trade with the Near East was being carried through the port of İzmir. This corresponded to over half of total Ottoman trade with Europe.[107] After suffering temporary setbacks during the Napoleonic Wars and the Greek War of Independence, the trade of İzmir regained its vitality in the 1830s. Between the 1840s and the 1870s the rate of expansion of commercial activity reached unprecedented levels when the total volume of trade of İzmir increased by four times, exports by three times, and imports by six times (see Table 1). During the rest of the nineteenth century, İzmir was the leading port of export of the Ottoman Empire; and in imports it was second only to İstanbul (see Table 1). Also, some of the most important articles exported from the Ottoman Empire in the course of the nineteenth century (such as madder, valonia, cotton, grapes, opium, tobacco, silk, licorice, scammony, and gall nuts) were either grown in the hinterland of İzmir or were brought there from the neighboring provinces.

In addition to its importance in the foreign trade of the empire, western Anatolia contained the wealthiest provinces of Anatolia, and as such it had always been a major contributor to the tax revenues of the Ottoman government.[108]

Structures of Agricultural Production and Elements of Integration

It is estimated that in the Ottoman Empire, under the conditions of the mid-nineteenth century, an average household of four to five people

TABLE 1

The volume of trade conducted at the main ports of the Ottoman Empire during the nineteenth century (Current £000)

	Early 1840s		1873–1877		1900s	
	Import	*Export*	*Import*	*Export*	*Import*	*Export*
İzmir	800	1250	3700	4300	2700	4000
Trabzon	200	100	600	300	500	500
Samsun	150	150	400	300	500	700
İstanbul	(2,000)	(500)	(10,000)	(5000)	7400	2800
Salonika	125	125	1500	1600	2500	1400

Source: Issawi 1980, 82.

with a pair of oxen and with occasional outside help, could cultivate as much as 8 hectares of land. Accordingly, lands that were held in units of less than 8 hectares can be characterized as small holdings.[109] These constituted the typical units of production in western Anatolian agriculture during the second half of the nineteenth century. This was generally true for most of the other parts of Anatolia as well, although there were some variations in the average size of holdings and production relations.[110] The earliest estimates about the distribution of farms according to their size in the Anatolian provinces are from the 1840s. According to these,[111] 81% of cultivated lands were held in plots of less than 5.4 hectares (60 dönüms). In 1869, 82.5% of cultivated land was held in small holdings of an average size 6 to 8 hectares, comprising more than 80% of the peasant households.[112] According to one of the first agricultural surveys conducted in the Ottoman Empire, 81% of cultivated land was held in holdings of 4.5 hectares (50 dönüms) or less in 1907.[113]

There are no detailed figures about the distribution of landholdings in western Anatolia during the earlier period, but contemporary accounts suggest that the situation there was not different from the general picture summarized above.[114] In 1840, the British consul in Bursa mentioned "peasant holdings and family labor" as the prevalent form of farming in the vicinity of the town.[115] In 1842, the same consul stated that "it is the peasantry who are the producers on small tracts."[116] In 1857, the British consul in İzmir responded to a questionnaire by reporting that "farming, generally in Anatolia, is carried out by peasant proprietors."[117] In 1863, it was reported that "by far, the largest proportion of cultivated land [around İzmir] is owned by peasants in farms of 3–20 acres (1.2–8 hectares)."[118] In the same year, a little to the north in Dardanelles, there were over ten thousand farms of less than four hectares.[119] In 1890, the average size of farms in all of Anatolia is calculated to be 1.2–4.8 hectares.[120] Available data is somewhat more complete for 1909 and indicates a continuation of the same pattern (see Table II). In other words, during the middle decades of the nineteenth century the expansion of agricultural exports was not accompanied by a marked tendency towards the centralization of landholdings in western Anatolia.

In one respect, the prevalence of small holdings in Anatolia can be traced back to the classical period of the Ottoman Empire. The mid-nineteenth century, however, is separated from the earlier period by an interval when local notables enlarged their properties. But the low population density made it difficult for them to find a steady supply of

TABLE 2
Distribution of land in Western Anatolia, 1909

Locality	Average Size of Farms in Hectares	0–5 Ha. %	Over 5 Ha. %
Karassi	5.4	78	22
İzmir	4.5	54	46
Bursa	2.3	75	25
Biga	2.0	70	30
İzmit	2.7	67	33
İstanbul	1.1	78	22
Bolu	2.0	85	15
Avg. for the Region	2.5	72	28

Source: Nickoley, 1924: 296.

laborers and threatened the continuing cultivation of their holdings.[121] For the most part, the work force they had access to was composed of peasants who owned small plots of land themselves and were willing to work on others' plots to supplement their incomes.[122] Alternatively, itinerant Lazes and Kurds from east central Anatolia circulated in and out of the region seasonally in search of employment.[123] Depending on the circumstances, the wealthier of the ayan could afford to pay the relatively high wages and tap such sources.[124] Local resources were so inadequate that in one instance, Karaosmanoğlu, who was the most important ayan in the area, organized the importation of "many" laborers from Morea to work on his fields in the 1770s.[125] But for the most part, leasing of large properties to peasant households in small plots under various forms of tenancy became the most common form of land use even during the heyday of the ayan's domination of the Anatolian countryside.[126] Thus, it would not be wrong to state that as far as the organization of agricultural production was concerned, the period of ayan represented a break more in form than in substance. Furthermore, the Anatolian ayan were much more likely to seek and obtain governmental posts than some of their counterparts in the Balkans. This can be seen as an attempt on their part to enhance the legitimacy of their claim over the rural surplus,[127] but in practice, acquiring governmental positions forced the ayan to turn into town-dwelling absentee landlords and diminished their ability to transform their rural property and wealth into a real basis of power. This in turn made them vulnerable to the counterattacks of the imperial center. Indeed, the imperial bureaucracy was able to undermine the power of the local notables in Anatolia within the span of a few years by unleashing against them the army that had been mobilized for the war with Russia in 1828. Shortly thereafter, their large holdings were confiscated, the timar system was formally abolished, and the use of corvée was banned.[128]

In western Anatolia, some of the land that was thus freed from the control of local ayan became the property of peasant households in small parcels.[129] Some continued to be leased to tax farmers as large estates, but since scarcity of labor continued as a problem, these estates too were broken down into small units and leased to peasantry, or they were cultivated by peasant households under sharecropping arrangements.[130] Throughout the rest of the nineteenth century, large parts of Anatolian lands remained uncultivated. Western Anatolia was no exception to this. Writing in 1841, the British consul in İzmir mentions "extensive tracts of land lying waste because there is nobody to cultivate them."[131] In 1842, in Bursa, "large tracts of land owned by Ottoman subjects [were] being offered for sale at very low prices, but they [could] not be sold."[132] Again in Bursa in 1851, "Since the forbidding of corvée, some big estates [were] abandoned or left empty because their owners [did] not find it profitable to sow by using hired labour."[133] In the interior of western Anatolia in the early 1850s, Ubicini observed "Vast solitudes, broken at intervals by a few tents . . . pine or oak forests . . . and about nine or ten leagues apart, some villages."[134] In the 1890s, arable land was still "plentiful and close at hand around Ankara."[135]

In addition to the persistence of small peasant holdings and continuing underutilization of land, farming implements used in Anatolian agriculture were generally simple. Smaller plots were cultivated by a wooden plow pulled by two oxen, and spade, hoe, and sickle.[136] Occasional attempts to use heavier and more advanced equipment in larger units failed mainly because of prohibitive costs, weakness of draft animals, and lack of means and skill for repairs.[137] Lack of irrigation or any other means of protection made the Anatolian peasantry extremely vulnerable to erratic rainfall, epidemics, locusts, and other natural calamities. In 1852, following a bad harvest, it was reported from Bursa that "peasants mine the bark of trees and mix it with flour to make bread for their families."[138] The cotton crop for 1863 had been expected to be about 200,000 bales, but as result of attacks by locusts and heavy rains, the yield did not exceed 60,000 bales in that or the next year.[139] During the famine of 1874:

grain was scarce because of the previous poor harvest and because hungry peasants had eaten their seed supplies during the winter [and] nine-tenths of the livestock had perished from natural causes or slaughtering for food. Men starved in streets and died without burial. In the Kayseri district a camel forty days dead was torn apart by the hungry; when the governor ordered it buried, people dug it up and ate the rotting flesh, some dying in consequence.[140]

According to these descriptions, the 1850s and the 1860s, that is, the interval when export trade was flourishing in western Anatolia, was bounded on both ends by periods of economic hardship. The foregoing also suggests that the intervening boom came about mainly through the new orientation of existing structures. Somehow, hundreds of the units of production that were dispersed in the western Anatolian countryside were interwoven with commercial threads in a marketing network that was readily responsive to the opportunities in domestic and export markets. What is more, once conditions changed, this network unraveled as fast as it came into being, leaving Anatolian villages in the early 1870s confronted with one of their worst crises.

Separately or together, four factors could have contributed to the commercial integration of western Anatolian agriculture in the mid-nineteenth century. These were, the policies formulated by the central government and implemented by local officials; activities of foreign residents (capitalists and the representatives of foreign governments); local merchants; and peasants (both as proprietors and sharecroppers).

Government Policies and Local Officials. The legislation and concessions that were drafted and granted under the rubric of Tanzimat were supposed to help regulate the social environment within which local groups were interacting. As such, when examined from a macro perspective, they can be seen as having at least the potential of contributing to the commercial integration of the structures of production and trade in the Ottoman Empire. But in their application, these policies encountered significant problems on the local level, and in many cases they created as much confusion as they paved the way for a consistent progress toward their purported aims.

Here, the main problem was that the principal motive behind the government's involvement in Anatolian agriculture was not to cause an increase in trade or production but to generate sufficient revenue to meet increasing state expenditures. But without the classical mechanisms of checks and balances that had served to protect imperial resources and the peasantry, this renewed emphasis on revenue generation made taxation increasingly oppressive in its methods and demands. Bureaucrats held on to tax farming as the most expedient method of collecting the tithe and converting it into cash. As a result, agricultural taxation was reduced to a relationship between the tax farmer and the cultivator in which the government intervened only ineffectually and sporadically.[141] In 1840, departing from the classical policy of maintaining differential rates for the tithe, the government introduced the uniform rate of one-tenth as applicable in all the provinces.[142] The main purpose of this measure was to simplify taxation procedures and its accounting. However, it had the unforeseen consequence of shifting the burden of taxation toward those sections of the peasantry whose holdings yielded proportionally less than those with better situated, more fertile lands.[143] Also, by the nineteenth century, government policy about the mode of collecting the taxes had become unclear. When collection in money was enforced (as was becoming increasingly the case), the peasantry was pressured to convert its crops into cash; this meant that peasants would frequently dispose of their crop on disadvantageous terms. On the other hand, when the tithe was collected in kind, the classical one day limit on the distance the peasants could be asked to travel in bringing their produce was violated by tax farmers. More important, the prevailing uncertainty at the level of the government gave the tax farmers, their subordinates, and their agents the liberty to insist on whichever form of collection was most favorable in terms of the market conditions, a situation that almost always worked to the detriment of the peasantry.[144]

Together with the sheep tax (*ağnam*), and other surtaxes, agriculture was contributing close to 50% of the revenues of the Ottoman government between the 1850s and the 1870s.[145] Within this sector, the overwhelming burden of taxation was on the direct cultivators.[146] Furthermore, the apportionment of local surtaxes within a region involved disproportionalities, as is described in the following account from 1845: "Wealthy and prosperous [İzmir] is taxed at 1,200,000 piastres. It has 30,000 houses. Menemen's tax with 1800 houses is half as much as [İzmir's]; whereas it should not be more than 72,000 piastres."[147] It was difficult for the peasantry to meet such demands. To avoid government pressure, they abandoned their lands and moved frequently. As a result of such dislocations, the number of houses in Menemen declined from 2,400 to 1,800 in the ten years between 1835 and 1845.[148] In the vicinity of Bursa, in an adverse season in 1852, peasants had to sell everything, "including clothing, copper kitchen utensils, ornaments, etc.," in order to meet their obligations.[149]

Military levies, by undercutting the already meager supply of labor, heightened the destructive effects of excessive taxation. According to the estimates by the British consul in Bursa, a conscription campaign undermined on the average the economic viability of one out of every four peasant households.[150] During the first half of the nineteenth century, frequent wars made the situation so oppressive that women in the countryside resorted to abortion and infanticide to relieve themselves of the burden of raising another child. "To what purpose bring up sons," one peasant complained, "as soon as they come to an age to be able to help us, [they] are liable to be taken away by conscription."[151] Thus, in western Anatolia, government taxation policies were more retrogressive than progressive in that they failed to create a more equitable and less abusive system and, indirectly, worsened the situation by leading to the further depopulation of the countryside.

A local perspective also reveals that the judicial reforms that took so much of the efforts of the Tanzimat statesmen did not penetrate deep enough in regional social structures to bring about significant change. The imperial edicts were quite insistent that local officials had to treat non-Muslim subjects justly,[152] but the central government did not have either the intention or the means to follow these orders. Records of local courts contain numerous entries suggesting that the position of non-Muslims before the Ottoman courts continued to be quite tenuous throughout the nineteenth century.[153] Even in cases where the conflict was exclusively among non-Muslims, they were rarely accepted as reliable witnesses. In court documents their names continued to be qualified with defamatory descriptions.[154] In resolving conflicts among non-Muslims and especially in dividing the estate of deceased persons, Islamic principles that favored the division of property were routinely applied by Ottoman courts.[155]

In analyzing the part played by the Ottoman government in the commercial integration of western Anatolia, we should also examine the effects of two kinds of policies that targeted specific crops. First were a series of surtaxes which the government imposed on the trade of spirits, cotton, wool, currants, madder, angora wool, silk, and opium between the 1790s and 1830s.[156] The government was planning to use this new revenue in financing the reorganization of its military and administrative institutions. In addition to these, a general tax on earnings (*iktisab*) was also imposed specifically in areas of active commerce like western Anatolia.[157] Together, these duties became the mainstay of the purchasing monopolies which the government set up in the early nineteenth century.[158] But rather than enhancing the government's role in the commercial integration of western Anatolia, these impositions helped further the influence of tax farmers as both the duties and the monopolies were farmed out soon after their imposition. The second set of policies seemed to actually support the production of some of these crops. For example, in the early 1860s, cultivators of cotton were exempted from the tithe, the rate of export duties was fixed for ten years, imported machinery was exempted from tariffs, and the better quality seeds imported from Egypt and the United States were distributed to the peasantry free of charge.[159] However, these stipulations were somewhat late in coming. The possibility of extending the cultivation of cotton in western Anatolia, to compete with American cotton, was mentioned for the first time on December 13, 1861, in an article in the semiofficial Istanbul daily *Ceride-i Havadis*. Then it had already been four years since the Manchester Cotton Supply Association sent its first question-naire on this topic to the British consul in İzmir,[160] and three years since the first shipment of sixty boxes of cotton seed from England landed in Izmir for distribution on the islands of Rhodes and Cyprus.[161] Later in the century, similar policies of support for grapes and silk were drafted by the government.[162] But like most reforms of the Tanzimat era, either these programs were never implemented on the local level, or when they were, this was done in such a haphazard manner that they were of little substantive consequence.[163]

The Ottoman policy of settlement was an example of government efforts that were directed at easing the labor shortage in Anatolia. During the nineteenth century, various groups and refugees from other parts of the empire, as well as from outside of it, were given land and settled in Anatolia, especially in the western parts.[164] Among these were Al-banians from Salonika in 1846;[165] Circassians from east-central Anatolia in 1846 and 1864;[166] Wallachians in 1849;[167] and Hungarians, following the invasion of Hungary by the Habsburgs in 1850.[168] Also, Bulgarian immigrants are frequently mentioned in the contemporary documents for their expertise in fruit growing around İzmir,[169] and Moldavians and Wallachians for their skills as engineers, surveyors, and supervisors in the construction of roads in the area.[170] The extent and the effect of this government-sponsored influx of people into western Anatolia is difficult to assess. According to one estimate, close to one million people immigrated to the Ottoman Empire between the 1850s and the 1890s.[171] Of these, the majority were Crimeans and Circassians. It is not clear how many of these were settled in western Anatolia, but a detailed breakdown of the population of İzmir province in 1893 indicates that of the 1,410,424 inhabitants, 1,050 were categorized as Latin Catholics, consisting mostly of the recent immigrants from the Balkans; a mere 415 were categorized as Bulgarians.[172] On the basis of these figures, and by taking into account the considerable outflow that occurred during the successive wars with Russia and Greece, it is fair to conclude that government policies of settlement do not seem to have significantly improved the population/land ratio to have an impact on the forms of production in agriculture.

Of the governors who served in İzmir during the first three quarters of the nineteenth century, only a few displayed the commitment and drive that would be necessary for the central government to become an effective force in the commercial integration of western Anatolia. During most of the first half of the nineteenth century, various members of the Karaosmanoğlu family managed to hold the important governmental posts amongst themselves.[173] During the second half of the nineteenth century, the government tried to recentralize provincial administration by frequently rotating its local officials. This led to a very high turnover rate especially among the governors. Only between 1858 and 1872 eighteen different governors served in İzmir.[174] Of these, İşkodralı Mustafa Pasha, who served in 1858, and Rıza Pasha, who served in 1861, were both over eighty years old at the time of their appointment. In 1860, another governor, Kayserili Ahmet, had to resort to employing a group of Albanian irregulars in order to suppress the bands of Zeybeks who were raiding the caravans in the hinterland. But these mercenaries preferred to engage in acts of plunder themselves rather than functioning as an arm of the local government.[175] Among eighteen governors, we can point out only two who approached their duties in a manner that was more in tune with the long-term needs of their province. One of these is Ahmet Pasha who, upon arriving in İzmir in 1863, issued a proclamation that included regulations concerning public safety, general hygiene, and standards of commercial practice.[176] The other is Rifat Efendi, who in 1867, established a school for the purpose of teaching orphan children of all denominations the different trades such as tailoring, shoe making, printing, and carpet making.[177] However, the general problem of brief tenure prevented these individuals from becoming truly effective as well since neither of them served for more than one year in their posts.

There is no doubt that the government policies enacted during the second half of the nineteenth century accommodated and facilitated the ongoing integration of Anatolian agriculture into the capitalist world economy. But by themselves, and especially with such limited means of implementation, they lacked a systematic cohesiveness to be the main force behind the commercial integration of a region such as western Anatolia.

Foreign Residents. After the turn of the nineteenth century, reduced duties, diminished supervision by the government, and the expanding scope of extraterritorial protection and jurisdiction made western Anatolia one of the most attractive and promising areas for foreign mercantile concerns in the Ottoman Empire. During the first half of the nineteenth century, there was an influx of foreigners into western Anatolia, multiplying the already substantial number of foreigners, especially in İzmir. In 1847, their number (including their families) was around 17,500.[178] At that time, the population of İzmir is estimated to be about 100,000.[179] In 1860, of 123,787 people living in İzmir, 28,352 were foreigners.[180] Within the next thirty years, both the population of İzmir and the number of foreigners living there had doubled, reaching 229,615 and 50,000, respectively in the late 1880s.[181] The breakdown of the foreign population for the two years for which we have data is shown in Table 3.

In addition to these, there was a large and increasing number of people who were granted the protection of foreign consuls by virtue of their business dealings with the nationals of these states. In the course of the nineteenth century, the privilege of issuing berats was

TABLE 3
Foreign population of İzmir in 1847 and 1860

	1847 (1)	1860 (2)
Greek	6800	15000
Austrian	4000	3150
British		
English	206	1200
Maltese	422	750
Ionian	3888	3500
French	712	546
Russian	180	50
Italian	572	3000
Other (3)	804	1156
Total	17584	28352

(1) Figures in FO 195/288:11, 18 February, 1847 are multiplied by 2 and rounded off.
(2) Farley 1862, 79–80.
(3) Includes Dutch, American, Persian, Scandinavian, Prussian.

widely abused by the consuls and their employees and there developed a brisk market in buying and selling of not only berats but also of foreign passports.[182] Naturally most of these transactions were not recorded. Therefore, it is difficult to have an accurate estimate of the number of people who were protected by various consulates as opposed to proper foreign citizens. In 1860 in İzmir, for example, it is reported that there were 314 people protected by the French, 60 by the Austrian, 60 by the Italian, and only 1 by the British consul.[183] No person of such status was reported by the Greek consulate. However, other documents from the period indicate that the Greek consulate, especially in İzmir, was very active in selling passports and that the Greek passports were very much in demand because they were easily exchanged for their Russian counterparts.[184] Overall, it seems that the granting of indiscriminate protection was prevalent among the representatives of lesser powers, such as Greece. Stronger states, especially the British, were reluctant to overextend such protection. The British government was even uncomfortable about the status of the large number of Ionians around İzmir, who by virtue of their islands being under British rule, were entitled to protection by the British state until 1862.[185]

The main reason for British reluctance was that during the first half of the nineteenth century the British community was more interested in extending its own operations in the hinterland of İzmir than in cooperating with or protecting local groups. Liberalized conditions in the area had opened up new possibilities for them. They formed a closely knit community around their consul and started to explore their chances.[186] They pressed the Ottoman administration to further expand the limits of extraterritoriality, and at the same time they were competing with the established merchants of the interior to create their own marketing network. One of their first initiatives in this respect was the establishment of a bank in İzmir. For reasons of safety, the founders of this institution took an unusual step and applied to the British government for a royal charter in 1843. The Commercial Bank of Smyrna was chartered in 1843 and operated until 1847.[187] Also in 1843, some of the leading British merchants in İzmir started the Smyrna Bank under the protection of the Swedish embassy.[188]

In the meantime, the influence of the representatives of the British state on the Ottoman officials grew in line with the improving relations between the two governments. Foreign merchants routinely solicited the intervention of the consuls on their behalf and took advantage of this leverage. Occasionally, Ottoman merchants also sought the support of the consuls when they were in a disagreement with the government officials, as did the ten Muslim subjects who in 1840 petitioned the British consul in İzmir to secure the reimbursement of 21,530 kuruş that was owed to them by the tax collector.[189] More interesting still is the case of the governor of İzmir who, upon receiving orders from Istanbul to assume the governorship of Konya, pleaded with the British consul to use his influence with the Ottoman court via the embassy in İstanbul to see to it that this appointment was reversed. The British consul was successful in obtaining this reversal.[190] British consuls tended to stay at their posts longer than Ottoman officials, which gave them an important advantage over the latter. For example, Consul Brant stayed in İzmir for 27 years, until his death in 1856.[191] In 1872, Consul Cumberbatch complained that, during the eight years he had been residing in İzmir, he had had to deal with "no less than twelve governors."[192]

Over the years, while the economic and the political presence of the British was becoming well entrenched in İzmir, their hopes of expanding that presence into the countryside did not materialize in any significant way. The Commercial Bank of Smyrna, which was to be one of the most important harbingers of such an expansion, ceased operations in 1847.[193] Similarly, none of the investments in the productive enterprises, such as the olive oil presses or cotton mills, lasted long enough to be of any significance.[194]

Potentially, granting foreigners the right to own private property was important in that it could lead to the establishment of mechanized agriculture in large estates by foreign residents outside the purview of the bureaucracy. There were a number of such attempts in western Anatolia,[195] but with the scarcity of labor and the resultant high wages, it was difficult to engage in large scale cultivation in a profitable manner. Indeed, soon after purchasing large tracts of land, some of the foreigners went bankrupt; others either left the property vacant, or leased it out to peasants in small units.[196]

As late as 1889, of the 55,467 foreigners living in all of western Anatolia, 50,009 were still residing in İzmir.[197] All British consuls and vice consuls were located either on the Aegean littoral or on the islands. The only consulate in the interior was in Bursa, and the holder of this post was demoted to the status of vice consul after the death of Consul Sandison in 1868. In his last report in 1867, Consul Sandison reported that only five British subjects were registered with the consulate.[198]

Whenever they had the opportunity, both British merchants and their consuls pointed at the absence of branch banking as the main impediment to the development of their businesses in western Anatolia. As we have seen, the few attempts to improve this situation stopped short of taking root in the region. Even the opening of a branch office of the Imperial Ottoman Bank in İzmir in 1868 failed to bring about any major change. Consul Cumberbatch complained that "the Bank appear[ed] to enter too frequently into commercial undertakings to the detriment of the traders."[199] Indeed, the overall anarchy that characterized the financial situation in western Anatolia made it very risky and difficult, if not impossible, for a foreign firm to make long-term commitments in the area. Neither roads nor the communication network were adequate. The port of İzmir was expanded and a quay was built with largely French capital between 1868 and 1876, but this created friction between the British and the French about its use and the duties to be charged.[200] Britain initially led the way in investments in railways in western Anatolia. The first sixty-one miles of railroad connecting İzmir with Kasaba in the hinterland together with the eighty-one miles between İzmir and Aydın were opened in 1866. But given the dispersal of peasant holdings and settlements in the countryside, it would be inaccurate to posit a direct relationship between the limited construction of railroads and the increased volume of trade in western Anatolia. Even after the rail network expanded to cover more of Anatolia, the railroad companies (which remained under foreign control until the 1930s) limited themselves to transportation. They did not become nor did they hire purchasing agents. So, they were not in a position to coordinate the circulation of goods in western Anatolia by themselves.[201] In Anatolia, railroads never became so widespread as to completely replace old methods of transportation either. Goods still had to be brought to the terminals by camel caravans. As late as in 1905, *The Times* of London reported that "on busy days over 1000 camels waited near the Ankara station to unload their cargoes."[202] The riders of these camels were mostly of the nomadic Yörük tribes who fully exploited their importance in the network of transportation.[203]

   In addition to such material difficulties, the conflicting interests of foreign merchants and local intermediaries created further barriers for the foreigners who were trying to penetrate the Anatolian countryside. The conflict between the two led not only to quiet subversion but also to active resistance by local merchants who used their influence at local and administrative levels to stop the British from establishing themselves in the interior. Competition between the British and local interests was most vigorous during the 1840s and the 1850s. In 1841, the Greek primates in Ayvalık solicited and obtained a decree from the governor of İzmir requiring British merchants dealing in oil to furnish guarantees in immovable property or in cash for the tithe and other duties that were incumbent upon the producers.[204] In 1843, Consul Brant expressed his suspicion that the real force behind the order that closed down the Smyrna Bank was the Greek bankers who were established in İstanbul, "such as the Baltazzi Brothers" who would be adversely affected by the opening of a bank in the Ottoman Empire.[205] In 1844, the British vice-consul in Rhodes states that "local notables and primates . . . by intrigues and other illicit means prevent our merchants from carrying on a legal trade."[206] A British merchant wrote in 1849 that "the Kadı, his brother, the sarraf Christofi together with the governor . . . are . . . leagued together to drive out of the district British merchants."[207]

For all these reasons, foreign merchants could not establish direct control over the sites of production in western Anatolia. That their numbers continued to increase in the coastal areas can also be gauged from the number of merchant houses in İzmir. In 1848, there were thirty such establishments, some of them with branch offices in İstanbul, Marseilles, and Liverpool.[208] By 1889, their number had gone up to sixty-three.[209] These houses were important as shippers and receivers of Ottoman and European goods at the port of İzmir, but for transactions in the hinterland, they ended up relying on local marketing networks, which they had initially sought to displace. Foreign merchants had no direct control over this network beyond hiring some non-Muslim merchants as purchasing agents.

In their petition of 1843, the founders of the Commercial Bank of Smyrna had stated the following as one of their reasons for seeking to establish this institution:

> . . . the bank will also provide, by means of agencies and bills of exchange for the transmission of funds to and from the interior of the country which is now principally effected by the inefficient medium of specie sent in small amounts at a time the roads being too unsafe to risk large sums. This branch of trade now being too hazardous for the British merchant, is carried on by the natives who are better acquainted with the country and the means of safety.[210]

In 1873, Consul Cumberbatch listed a number of problems regarding the state of British trade in western Anatolia. Among them was the following:

Of late years, wealthy natives of the country have been in the habit of purchasing the produce by anticipation and selling it with heavy profit to merchants, thereby miming the producers by interest and low prices and shutting out the British merchant from the interior trade. The only remedy [would be] the establishment of district banks charging a low rate of interest.[211]

Even though thirty years had passed in between, the striking similarity between the problems mentioned in the two documents shows how little ground the British merchants had gained in achieving their original aims in western Anatolia.

Intermediaries. For any group to organize and be in charge of a marketing network in western Anatolia, it was essential to maintain some contact with peasant households in the hinterland. Within the context of the mid-nineteenth century western Anatolian agriculture, we can identify three kinds of activities that, while originating from outside of the rural areas, reached the peasantry. These were, first, the collection of the tithe; second, making the necessary arrangements for transportation of the tithe (if in kind) and/or the surplus product to the provincial towns and to the port of export; and third, lending money to the peasantry to help them meet their financial obligations. In some instances, these three activities were performed by three different groups, but on the local level, it was by far most common for the same individual or group to engage in trade, tax farming, and money lending at the same time. What enabled the same group of intermediaries to dominate all of these activites was the access they had to liquid funds which gave them a distinct advantage over government officials and foreign merchants. The concerns over security and the general budgetary problems of the Ottoman Empire prevented the latter two groups from injecting sufficient amounts of cash into regions like western Anatolia. As a result, most of the money that was used to purchase tax farming privileges, or to organize the trade of the region, originated from the coffers of the private banking firms in Istanbul. In the absence of a regulated financial environment in the Ottoman Empire, these firms had amassed fortunes through sophisticated methods of speculation and profiteering.[212] During the first half of the nineteenth century, as the need of the imperial bureaucracy for short-term loans increased, the private fortunes of the leading banking firms such as the Baltazzis, the Rallis, the Zarafis, the Rodoconachis, and the Düzüoğlus multiplied.[213] Most of these family firms had formidable links with commercial and financial circles in

Europe as well. For example, the Ralli Brothers, in 1865, had offices in London, Manchester, Marseilles, Istanbul, Tabriz, Odessa, and St. Petersburg.[214] They were also bringing their resources together and creating centralized financial structures in İstanbul. Originally, private bankers (*sarrafs*), who were accredited by the Ottoman government, were organized in a corporate body that, in the early 1840s, had eighty members. As their activities became larger and more sophisticated, their numbers declined, and were reduced to eighteen by the mid-1850s.[215] Starting with the İstanbul Bankası (The Bank of İstanbul) in 1845, these families played prominent roles in most of the major private and public banks that were established in the second half of the nineteenth century. This created an interlocking structure of partnership that included not only the leading local families but also major European financiers such as Paris Credit Mobilier and Société Generale.[216]

The centralization of money capital in this fashion meant that tax-farming privileges were repeatedly being purchased by the same few firms in İstanbul. Or, alternatively, the same few firms were acting as the guarantors to the purchasers of tax farms.[217] The tax farmer, after purchasing his privileges in İstanbul, would either send in his agents to collect the tithe directly or,more commonly, he would go through a number of intermediaries with successive subcontracts, as described by Consul Sandison in 1857: "The government contractors who farm [local tithes] from the Porte . . . usually resell detached portions [for] a profit. The product in kind or in money is made over to the sarraf [who had lent to the local purchaser] in pledge and repayment of his advances."[218] Through such transactions, the sarrafs, who were already acting as merchants and money-lenders, increasingly acquired the further role of tax farmer and tithe collector in their localities. Where the tax farmer and the sarraf remained separate, the former was almost always subordinated to the latter through the complex network of indebtedness that operated both in Istanbul and in the particular province. In other words, bearers of circulating capital were playing an important role in determining the scope and rhythm of commercial activites in western Anatolia. Consequently, mercantile interests were relegated to a secondary position, and for all practical purposes the government had become dependent on these same circles for financing its own day-to-day operation.

As far as the peasants were concerned, there could not have been any question regarding the legality or propriety of the intermediary activities. After all, what was being demanded of them was the ancient tithe, and it hardly made any difference if it was collected by government officials or by tax farmers.[219] However, as the nineteenth century progressed, the intermediary groups acquired more effective ways of squeezing the peasantry who, in the face of declining government control, had neither a recourse nor any means of resisting.

For example, Ottoman laws stipulated that no crop should be marketed unless it could be proven that its tithe was already paid. The tax farmer would usually evaluate the crops, determine the amount of tithe that was due on them, and contract the crops while they were still on the ground. Then, if the market was favorable at the time of the harvest, he would promptly collect the tithe and the remaining crop, and secure a profitable return for this initial outlay. If, however, the market was not favorable, he would delay his tours in the countryside, postponing the completion of the transaction, sometimes for months. In the meantime, the crops would be deteriorating in the fields. When he finally arrived, he would insist on collecting the pre-assessed tithe in money; which, in real terms, would amount to two to three times the legal rate set by the government. After this, peasants could not do much with their crops except dispose of them at low prices and in the end become ever more indebted to the tax farmer. Such irregularities are described as pervasive in the 1830s, 1850s, and 1870s by Urquhart, Ubicini, and Consul Cumberbatch, respectively. Urquhart says, for example, that

> bankers obtain . . . the order for collecting the revenue before harvest time. By anticipating the time of payment, the bankers receive two and a half percent interest per month on the money which the peasant is obliged to borrow; depress the market after the harvest by the necessity in which the peasant is placed of realizing, as the condition of the loan; bargain with the villages for the exclusion of all other competitors for the produce, and even for a reduction of the price below that of the then depressed market.[220]

Ubicini notes that

> the peasant . . . goes to the nearest town, where he borrows the sum that he requires, on condition of paying back what has been advanced, in corn, subsequently and at a rate agreed upon beforehand. This rate is commonly from five to six piastres the *kile*, whilst after the harvest he could easily obtain from nine to ten

piastres. Thus, the produce of his fields which is only just sown is sold to another at a loss of from 30 to 40 percent.[221]

Cumberbatch observes that

[the value of the crop is assessed] when green or not until it is over ripe . . . whereby it frequently occurs from bad weather the ped does not arrive at maturity or that much of the ripe cotton is blown away, the farmer being prohibited from picking it until the demands of the tithe collector are satisfied, which individual assumes the right of estimating when he pleases.[222]

The widespread practice of tax farming and the pervasive nature of informal credit gave the sarrafs the power to affect all sorts of economic activities in western Anatolia. As early as 1842, Ralli Brothers was reported to have maintained purchasing agents in the interior of Bursa and İzmir throughout the year.[223] In addition to acting as purchasers, these agents were also creating funds for their parent establishment. Even when the merchants were formally independent of the bankers, they were still tied to the sources of credit through a complex network of interchanges which had to accommodate, among other things, the seasonal requirements: the import trade in İzmir took place in March, April, and June; importers then would be in need of paper money to remit to Europe; as export trade at that period would be small, a considerable demand for paper money would take place in the area. At the same time, domestic merchants also required funds to send into the interior for the purchase of produce. When that produce began to come to markets in July and was being bought for export, paper money would be more abundant. In the absence of branch banking in the area, private bankers in Istanbul or their agents would step in. They would sell drafts in the first half of the year, and purchase for remittance in the second.[224] Such links with İstanbul, which were structural and permanent, made the local economy extremely vulnerable to the fluctuations in the money markets of Galata and even of Europe.[225]

An incident reported by Consul Brant in 1849 demonstrates the extent of the controlling power these firms had established over Anatolian commerce. An Armenian sarraf in Istanbul advanced a loan of 800,000 *kuruş* to the chief of a nomadic Yörük tribe named Cihanbeyli. Not being able to recover the loan, the sarraf sold it to another firm who for five years added compound interest to the original sum. In the fall of 1849, the Cihanbeyli tribe came to İzmir to collect their dues from the various butchers to whom they had sold livestock. At that time, the governor of İzmir, Osman Efendi, received orders from İstanbul to compel the butchers to pay to him the amount that was due to the Yörüks. The butchers complied, and the governor, upon collecting the money, transmitted it to İstanbul, where it was used to settle the sarraf's account.[226] There is other evidence of the pervasive influence of the financiers in the region: In 1848 the customs of the Asiatic Coast, from the southern entrance to the Bosporus to the confines of Egypt had been purchased by an Armenian sarraf at the capital; and the tithes had been purchased by another, in most of Bursa province and "all of various *paşalıks* adjacent to it."[227] In the seventeenth and eighteenth centuries, the members of the same Jewish family held the post of opium broker in İzmir.[228] In addition to trade and dealing in money, the intermediary firms occasionally extended their activities into farming and manufacturing enterprises such as cloth making, steam mills, mines, and lines of steamboat and communications.[229] In 1851, "one very large estate fell in debt to a wealthy Armenian sarraf in İstanbul. It [was] run on his account by a manager" in Bursa.[230] In 1856, "[O]ne very extensive land proprietor and mercantile speculator in conjunction with an Anglo-Greek house at the capital, . . . erected the largest filature of any on his property near [Bursa], added to it a spacious building for lodging his factory girls and other workers and for rearing silk worms. He produced cocoons of unrivaled quality."[231] It was reported the same year that the only regular steam line between Gemlik (near Bursa) and İstanbul belonged to a company of Armenian sarrafs.[232]

However, the real fulcrum of power of these intermediaries was their money dealing. It was through the large credit network that they controlled economic activities in western Anatolia and acquired a leverage with the political authorities in the region and in İstanbul. At the capital, sarrafs acted as the confidantes of the higher bureaucrats, conducting their financial affairs and advancing money when it was needed.[233] Their influence on local administrators was substantial as well. Especially prior to the institution of regular salaries in 1839, newly appointed governors were required to post a sum of money as security for the taxes they would be collecting in their localities. This sum, which sometimes was as high as 500,000 kuruş, was usually advanced by a sarraf who would charge interest at about 2% per month. An agent of the sarraf would accompany the pasha to his province as his personal banker. "All money transactions would pass through his hands; and the agiotage (a premium that was imposed as a safeguard against the declining value of Ottoman coins) and commissions charged by him were considerable. This agent received the revenue of the province, for which his principal [had] become responsible, and trafficked in its produce which he [managed] to obtain at reduced price. . . ."[234] Venality in government offices and with it the influence of the sarrafs continued well after the reorganization of provincial administration in 1852. As late as 1872, a discharged custom house clerk was appointed to the presidency of Criminal Tribunal in İzmir because he had purchased the office.[235]

Even more serious than these was the indebtedness of the government treasury to these private bankers. Prior to the raising of the first European loan in 1856, the Ottoman government had issued a series of public bonds and a quasi-paper money, called *kaime,* both of which were either purchased or eventually discounted by the Galata firms. In addition to these, the banking firms routinely extended credit directly to the treasury.[236] According to some estimates, in 1860, the short-term debts of the various government offices to private banking firms alone amounted to 250 million francs.[237] It was probably as a result of such financial transactions between the Palace and the bankers that Sultans Abdülmecit and Abdülaziz spent most of their time in the Christian sections of İzmir when they visited the city. In 1850, Abdülmecit stayed in İzmir for one day and spent most of it "visiting a Armenian sarraf in the adjacent village of Bornova."[238] Similarly, in 1863, Sultan Abdülaziz greatly disappointed the Muslim population of the city when he visited the Turkish quarters only after the fifth day of his stay in İzmir. In the meantime he had paid a call to the Whittalls and dined with the Baltazzis.[239]

The intermediate group could use their influence in the economic and political circles of the Ottoman Empire to avert risks and secure profits for their investments. The diversity of their activities gave them the opportunity to shift their funds among the different fields and, if necessary, summon the active support of the domestic and/or foreign officials. Owing to their pervasive influence, their decisions had a bearing on the overall direction of economic activities in regions like western Anatolia. Typically, the intermediary group as a whole had four avenues for generating profit. These were tax farming, money-lending, money-changing, and trade. Farming of taxes was in itself an extremely lucrative operation for the purchasers of these grants. According to Consul Brant, in 1850 the right to levy certain surtaxes in the province of Aydın was sold for 490,000 kuruş in all, and the revenue generated from these sources was no less than 5,000,000 kuruş.[240] According to Ubicini, in the early 1850s "the [farmer] of Customs in the town of B . . . . who had received it [at 1,500,000 piastres] cleared a net profit of 1,000,000 piastres."[241] It was also common for the bidders in auctions to amass profits by reselling the tithe farms on the day they purchased them. In one such instance, the original purchaser is reported to have made an instant "gain of 1.8 million piastres by the subselling of about 2 million piastres worth of tithes."[242]

The second source of profit for the bankers and their agents was the high interest they collected from the short-term loans they routinely extended to merchants and farmers. Although there were regional and conjunctural variations, the informal credit market operated on the basis of 20%–25% interest per annum throughout the empire during the third quarter of the nineteenth century.[243] In 1861, following the collapse of the Mires loan,[244] in Bursa, "frequently 1/4 to 1/2 percent a day [was] paid for loans in gold, . . . whilst 2.5 to 5 percent a month [were] more common rates."[245] In İzmir in 1863, "the normal rate [was] 1.5 to 2 percent a month; calculated in most instances as compound interest."[246] In the meantime, the government had set the legal rate of interest as 12% per annum applicable in all kinds of transactions across the empire. In the absence of a coherent banking policy and as a result of the continuing dearth of liquid funds, money-lending became even more widespread. Debt related cases constituted close to half of the 860 civil suits that were brought before the British Consular Court in İzmir between 1858 and 1860. The sum of money involved in these cases exceeded £24,000, over £17,000 of which pertained to cases of simple loans between private individuals.[247] The bureaucracy did not have the necessary means or the power to either control the informal credit market or to enforce a universal rate upon these transactions. In fact, occasional intervention by the government to end fiscal anarchy and to reform the financial organization of the empire, provided the intermediaries with a third source or profit.

For one thing, borrowing from Europe brought little improvement to provincial financial disarray because little if any of this money found its way into the provinces. The Ottoman Bank opened up branch offices but failed to fulfill the expectations that were placed in it. As far as financial institutions were concerned, there was little, if any, change or improvement in the provinces. As for purely monetary matters, no clear universal standard was established for exchanging the various types of money that were circulating in the provinces. This situation opened endless possibilities of profit for the intermediary group of tax farmer/merchant/sarrafs. In collecting the farmed taxes they could determine the mode of collection (i.e., in kind or money) and they could also demand payment in a specific currency. Since the intermediaries were also the sole source for exchanging the money the public happened to have at the moment, the peasantry sometimes ended up paying two to three times the prescribed rate in making up the difference between the current value of the coins and the paper. Also, the multiple connections of the sarrafs enabled them to corner huge profits by taking advantage of the disparities between the current rates in Istanbul and in the provinces.[248] In 1854, the government tried to ban the circulation of kaime in the provinces, but because of the inadequate supply of metallic money, coins started to circulate at a 20%–25% premium in Bursa, enabling the sarrafs to mediate in a series of profitable transactions between Bursa and İstanbul.[249] In 1858, kaime was prohibited once again and the rate of exchange was set at 100 kuruş = 1 mecidiye. After a forty-day period, the older transactions that had been carried out under the paper money at 120 kuruş–140 kuruş were to be cleared according to the new rate. This involved a "great disorder and injustice to debtors, especially to the peasantry indebted to the sarrafs. The difference between the two rates meant a 30 percent mark-up in the sarrafs' receivables."[250] The government insisted on banning the kaime, but in the absence of a suitable replacement it continued to be used, albeit at a discount of 15%–25%. The beşliks, which the government was trying to establish as the legal tender, were so debased that they hardly fetched half of their intrinsic value.[251] In 1859, there were still four different kinds of kuruş in use in most of western Anatolia. First, that in beşlik money receivable for taxes at 112 kuruş–114 kuruş = 1 Mecidiye; second, kaime exchangeable in İstanbul at 150 kuruş–160 kuruş = 1 Mecidiye; third, a conventional currency in trade, at 140 kuruş = 1 Mecidiye; fourth, the issue rate of 1 Mecidiye at 100 kuruş par.[252] Depending on the transaction, the sarrafs provided the right type of currency at the appropriate places, profiting from the discrepancies among these different units.

Local officials of the government, sometimes on behalf of the central bureaucracy but more often on their own behalf, were also profiting from the fiscal anarchy. In 1849, they were reported to be collecting the taxes in the interior in specie which they either hoarded, or disposed of in İzmir at high rates, or exported abroad.[253] Later in 1852, "those who had no other money than gold sovereign taken at 120 kr. had to exchange them by a sarraf at 110–118 kr. or tender them at that rate to the authorities who reissued the coin at its full value for their own benefit."[254] In 1858, the Porte demanded that the customs on silk should be paid in Gemlik rather than in İstanbul because the government note that was valued at 20 kuruş in İstanbul was valued at 16 kuruş in

Gemlik.[255] As these examples show, the discord that existed among the value of the various units of exchange in the same or different locations made arbitrage and dealing in money in general an extremely profitable activity.

The conditions that made tax-farming, money-lending and money-changing lucrative venues of investment rendered trade and long-term planning in production and commerce very risky and unattractive. In the absence of a universal equivalent, it was often impossible to determine or predict the prices of articles destined for domestic or foreign trade. For example, in Bursa, "for many articles two sets of prices developed; those in paper and those in beşliks, both of which were subject to violent fluctuations."[256] In terms of external trade, the depreciation in the nominal rate of exchange of kuruş with other currencies continued during the first half of the nineteenth century. In 1740, the pound was 5 kuruş–7 kuruş in İstanbul. In 1844, the rate had gone down to 111 kuruş.[257] In addition to this general decline, the regional disparities and seasonal fluctuations in the value of kuruş made coordination of export activity particularly difficult. Perhaps more important than the nominal depreciation of kuruş was its real depreciation resulting from continuous debasement. According to some reports, in 1854, 250 kuruş or more was required to yield the par in pure silver of a pound sterling.[258]

Given the uncertainties involved and compared to the relative ease of amassing fortunes by simple arbitrage, the intermediaries were normally reluctant to risk their fortunes in trade. As we will see in the next chapter, they coordinated their efforts with the export firms in İzmir and channeled their funds and efforts toward forming a commercial network rather than speculation only under the most profitable conditions of the 1850s and the 1860s. Otherwise the prevailing chaos was serving them well, and they did everything in their power not only to prevent foreigners from penetrating the hinterland but also to derail the government policies of fiscal reorganization.

Peasantry. As a type of ownership and cultivation, the small peasantry is dynamic enough to independently respond to market conditions and organize some of the commercial agriculture. When considered in relation to the labor requirements of the types of crops grown in western Anatolia, the suitability and advantage of this type of production becomes particularly clear. Poppies had to be incised one by one on the farm to extract opium from them.[259] Grapes had to be picked and treated with potash to convert them into raisins.[260] Cotton was picked and pressed into bales manually.[261] Other export crops, like valonia and madder roots, had to be extracted from the wild.

Depending on the particular crop, quite a few labor-saving methods were utilized in these small plots. For example, mulberry trees in Bursa were planted close to each other to prevent them from growing to full size. This made their leaves (which were used to feed silkworms) more accessible with less labor.[262] In 1844, in İzmir "farmers plant[ed] cotton and sesame on the same plot intermixed; because they require[d] similar care."[263] In this way, farmers were doubling their chances in the market. Again, in İzmir in 1863, local producers refused to plant imported Egyptian cotton seed, which was distributed to them free of charge, because it required more attention, hence more labor.[264] There was also the common practice of leaving the land fallow for one year in every 2–3 years on a rotating basis. This meant that the area that was under cultivation was larger than that which was actually cultivated in a given year.[265]

In addition to these, a relatively small number of peasants could cultivate and harvest more than one kind of crop in different plots because agricultural production in a given farm did not always require the same labor force in the course of a year.[266] Among other things, planting and harvesting times were different for different crops. Poppies were harvested in July; valonia in July and August; cotton between August and October; and grapes in September and December.[267] In a contemporary report from Bursa, it is indicated that in the 1850s, "usually reapers come from the higher country between Bursa and Kütahya; work and return there for that harvest which takes place two weeks after here."[268]

Finally, the range of activities in which women and children were employed expanded during the middle decades of the nineteenth century. This prompted the British consul to remark, "those [women] of the peasantry are active and laborious, performing much field and other heavy work in addition to their domestic duties, whilst the men may be loitering in idleness."[269]

The dispersed pattern of settlement in the Anatolian countryside, however, prevented the farming households from taking full advantage of the inherent dynamism of small peasant ownership. Only a fraction of the peasantry whose plots were located near towns could directly respond to market conditions and contribute independently to commercial agriculture. The rest were dependent on the intermediaries for all their needs, including the marketing of their crops. It was no coincidence that as the nineteenth century progressed, the export crops, like grapes and tobacco, became visibly concentrated around towns and especially in the vicinity of İzmir. Consequently, such lands came to be in high demand and were increasingly acquired by Greeks and Armenians.[270]

CONCLUSION

The peripheral status of the Ottoman territories was ultimately determined by the way in which the local networks of production and trade were transformed during the nineteenth century. Thousands of peddlers, store owners, petty bankers, as well as the bigger tax farmers, merchants, and bankers, played a crucial role in this transformation. More than the government policies or the penetration of foreign calital, it was the activities of this group of intermediaries that was responsible for the peripheral integration of the local networks in regions like western Anatolia. To some extent, the intermediaries were also responsible for curbing the effectiveness of the policies of reform articulated by the Ottoman government and for limiting the foreign (especially British) presence in the Anatolian countryside. These local groups owed most of their wealth and influence to the fiscal and administrative anarchy that reigned in the Ottoman Empire. While actively thwarting Ottoman and British attempts at fiscal reform, they also shunned long-term commitments to trade and investment, because profits to be obtained from changing all kinds of money were much superior and safer.

Another implication of these descriptions is that in western Anatolia no major expansion in production for European markets could take place without the initiative and active involvement of the intermediaries. On the other hand, given the patterns of ownership and methods of cultivation that prevailed in western Anatolia, the intermediaries could organize or participate in such a venture only if the expected returns from such a reorientation rose high enough to justify a diversion of funds from the other venues of easy profit. As we will see in the next chapter this is precisely what happened in the 1850s and the 1860s, when the demand for and prices of certain exports of the Ottoman Empire increased fast and high enough. This was enough of an incentive for the intermediaries to invest in trade and profit from it. But it meant that the ensuing boom occurred under their term, leading to the further enhancement of their status and hence the strengthening of the peripheral structures in the empire.

İzmir, 1845. From a daguerrotype taken on the roof of the governor's house. (*Illustrated London News*, VI–VII, August 9, 1845, p. 84.)

İzmir, 1853. From the Jewish cemetery. (*Illustrated London News*, XXIII, December 17, 1853, p. 512.)

Ceremonies celebrating the commencement of the İzmir-Aydin railway in İzmir on September 22, 1857. (*Illustrated London News*, XXXI, October 31, 1857, p. 436.)

A view of workers at the tobacco processing plant that was owned and operated by Regie des Tabacs in İzmir, ca. 1892. (Author's collection.)

Port of İzmir, ca. 1901. (Author's collection.)

Two views of the waterfront and the boardwalk in İzmir, ca. 1906. (Author's collection.)

A street in the Greek quarters of İzmir, ca. 1920. (Author's collection.)

4

Growth in the Periphery: Western Anatolia, 1840–1876

OTTOMAN AND WESTERN ANATOLIAN TRADE

The period between the 1840s and the 1870s was unique in the historical development of relations between the capitalist world economy and the Ottoman Empire. The growth of Ottoman exports exceeded that of her imports for the first and only time during this period. In western Anatolia, where the empire's main port of export was located, and from where most of its leading exports were derived, an absolute and significant growth occurred in the region's export surplus in the same years.[1] In the following pages, I will analyze the dynamics and consequences of this expansion by concentrating primarily on the commercial links between western Anatolia and the United Kingdom. Between the 1830s and the 1870s, Britain's share in the exports from the Ottoman Empire as a whole increased from 13.3% to 27.2%. Likewise, in the 1830s, Britain supplied 19.0% of Ottoman imports, and in the 1870s, 32.4%.[2] Other major trading partners of the Ottoman Empire in order of significance were France, Austria, Russia, and the United States. Among these, only the shares of France and Austria came significantly close to that of Britain. Between the 1840s and the 1860s, France especially, seemed to have regained the ground it had lost in Near Eastern trade following the Napoleonic Wars. But France's position in these years still did not match the 1780–90 period, when it accounted for one-half

87

to three-fifths of Ottoman trade with Europe.[3] Also, both French and Austrian trade figures tend to be overvalued, because the transit trade with Prussia, Belgium, Switzerland, and Spain were included in them.[4] In general, the developments in the trade of İzmir followed these trends closely. Britain's share in İzmir's trade increased from 30.8% to 43.5%, and that of France decreased from 42.1% in 1787 to 11% in 1874–78.[5]

The goods that were exported from the Ottoman Empire were mostly agricultural raw materials and foodstuffs, and, except for carpets and some silk fabrics and clothes, there were no manufactured exports.[6] Of the commodities exported to Britain, I shall pay particular attention to valonia, madder roots, raisins, opium, and cotton as a representative sample. Together, these articles constituted from 43% to 73% of total Ottoman exports to Britain between the 1840s and 1870s.[7] They were mostly produced within western Anatolia and were almost exclusively shipped from İzmir. Another important group of articles exported from the Ottoman Empire but not included in our tables are cereals and corn. Between 1860 and 1862, these constituted about 35.5% of British imports from the Ottoman Empire. Most of this, however, was exported from the Balkan provinces.[8] In western Anatolia, most of the cereal farming was done for local and household consumption. Exports occurred only when there was a seasonal surplus.[9] Availability of marketable surplus depended on local conditions, climate, and government policies that would occasionally ban such exports depending on imperial needs. Consequently, grain exports from Anatolia fluctuated from one year to the next and sometimes were totally reversed, with considerable imports coming from Russia and Eastern Europe.[10] Therefore, the occasional exports of cereals from western Anatolia between 1840 and 1876 do not necessarily indicate that the production processes in cereal farming were permanently linked to world markets.[11]

DEMAND

There were three reasons for the rise in demand for Ottoman exports during the mid-nineteenth century. The first of these relates to the general developments in the world economy. There was an overall increase in the demand for agricultural and raw materials from the periphery to supply the newly developing industries of Europe, an increase accentuated by the Crimean War and the American Civil War. Also under this heading mention should be made of the desire of the British government to balance its accounts in general, but especially with

TABLE 4

Trade of Izmir, annual averages in current mil. francs

Year	Total			Britain						France					
	Import	Export	Total	Import	%	Export	%	Total	%	Import	%	Export	%	Total	%
1839–1843	14.5	32.9	47.4	5.6	39	9.0	27	14.6	31	1.8	12	6.5	20	7.3	15
1844–1848[1]	12.5	20.0	32.5					14.1	43					5.6	17
1849–1853[2]	29.3	36.4	65.7					31.0	47					9.1[4]	14
1854–1858	55.8	56.3	112.1	21.9[2]	39	25.2[2]	44	47.1	42	9.2[3]	16	7.4[3]	13	16.6	15
1859–1863[3]	69.2	84.0	153.2	21.6[3]	31	42.6[3]	50	64.2	42	11.6[4]	17	10.7[4]	13	22.3	15
1864–1868[3]	54.6	107.1	161.7	16.2[2]	30	67.8[2]	63	84.0	52	11.8[3]	22	15.6[3]	15	27.4	17
1869–1873[4]	101.1	112.8	214.5	48.0[2]	47	43.0[2]	38	91.0	42	16.4[4]	16	11.8	10	28.2	13
1874–1878	90.2	103.4	193.5	41.0	45	43.2	41	84.2	44	13.0	14	8.4	8	21.4	11

Notes:
(1) Only 1846
(2) Average of three years
(3) Average of four years
(4) Average of two years

Source: My own calculations based on Georgiades 1885, 188–189, and Issawl 1980, 110.

peripheral areas with which it had been running an export surplus in the post-Napoleonic era. The second reason relates to the importance of the Near East and particularly of the Ottoman Empire in the establishment and continuation of British hegemony in the world economy. Increased exports from the empire would not only augment the income of Ottoman farmers and merchants but would also increase the tax revenues of the Ottoman state and hence contribute to its strength. Third, there were a number of developments that affected particular Ottoman exports. Valonia (large acorn cups of a species of oak) was valued for the tannin it contained and was used in making leather. In the seventeenth and eighteenth centuries, when leather manufacturing was at its height in the Ottoman Empire, most of the valonia was consumed locally. As late as the 1840s, valonia exports did not amount to more than 4% of total exports to the United Kingdom. With the development of competing tanneries in Europe, the manufacture of leather goods suffered a setback in the Ottoman Empire, and more of the valonia grown in western Anatolia were exported abroad. By the 1870s, the share of valonia in Ottoman exports to the United Kingdom had gone up to over 21%.[12]

Before the 1860s, the British textile industry was dependent on imported agricultural raw materials for dyeing and finishing. Madder root from around İzmir was valued very highly for its fast red coloring ("Turkish red") of all textiles.[13] During the 1860s and the early 1870s, alizarin, a synthetic dye derived from coal tar, was developed, and within less than twenty years it completely captured the market from natural dyes.[14] Consequently, the share of madder roots in the Ottoman exports declined from 41.5% in 1840–44 to a mere 5.0% in 1870–74, and completely disappeared thereafter.[15]

Prior to the nineteenth century, in Anatolia, opium was produced mostly for its medicinal power and was consumed locally. Its transformation into a cash crop and the concomitant expansion of its cultivation occurred through a number of stages in the nineteenth century. First among these was the growing involvement of the Americans in the opium trade between the Ottoman Empire and China. Americans were joined and eventually displaced by the British who made their first entry into this trade in 1834, when the monopolies of the East India Company were repealed. The abolishing of the Ottoman government monopoly over the trade of this article in 1838 removed the remaining constraints on the further commodification of the Ottoman opium. After a temporary setback during the Opium Wars, the Anatolian crop received another boost from the development of the pharmaceutical industries in Europe and the United States.[16] The area devoted to the cultivation of poppies in western Anatolia increased rapidly. The crop was 330,000 pounds in 1836; 418,000 pounds in 1866; and over 600,000 pounds in the 1870s. Concomitantly, the share of opium in Ottoman exports to the United Kingdom increased from 0.5% in 1840 to 14.0% in 1874.[17]

Cotton had been grown in western Anatolia and exported in large quantities long before the nineteenth century.[18] However, starting from the turn of the nineteenth century, cheaper and better quality cotton from the United States displaced Ottoman cotton, especially from the British markets. After these years, the share of cotton wool in Ottoman exports to Britain fell below 1%.[19] Cotton production in and exports from western Anatolia was reinvigorated during the middle decades of the nineteenth century when British textile manufacturers became interested in balancing their dependence on American cotton by developing alternative sources. The Manchester Cotton Supply Association was founded for this purpose in 1857.[20] British consuls abroad were questioned by the association about the possibilities of expanding the cultivation of cotton in their jurisdictions. From their response, western Anatolia appeared as one of the most promising areas.[21] Arrangements were made to encourage cotton cultivation and to send good quality American seed to such places. But the real boost to Anatolian cotton growing came with the American Civil War. Uncertainties about the future of American sources made the cotton cultivation in western Anatolia profitable. Between 1861 and 1862, the area devoted to cotton around İzmir expanded four times; and between 1862 and 1863, by a further two to three times.[22] During the war years, the annual crop increased over tenfold, from 12,000 to 150,000 bales.[23] By itself, cotton constituted over 50% of the value of total Ottoman exports to Britain in 1864. This, however, proved to be a temporary boom. Due to the agroeconomic conditions in western Anatolia, the inferior quality of cotton grown there, and the absence of steady support by the Ottoman government, both the cultivation and the export of cotton rapidly declined after the ending of the American Civil War. By the 1870–74 interval, the share of cotton in total Ottoman exports to Britain had declined to 6.6%. After the 1870s, exports to other places (most notably to Spain) continued on a small but regular basis.[24]

Increases in the exports of grapes and raisins occurred during the middle decades of the nineteenth century. This was partly related to the changing consumption habits in Europe, but the major push behind the increased demand for the products of Ottoman viticulture was the spread of phylloxera (a grapevine disease) in the United States and

Europe. Even though grapes were grown in most Ottoman provinces, those that were exported came exclusively from İzmir and Bursa.[25] Especially after the decline of cotton prices in the world markets, an increasing number of farmers turned their cotton fields into vineyards.[26] In the 1870s, production in the vicinity of İzmir, which contained one-fifth of all Ottoman vineyards, had reached 50,000 tons; half of this amount was exported.[27] In those years, raisins alone constituted more than 10 percent of the total Ottoman exports to Britain.[28] After the 1870s, barring a slowdown during the 1890s (due to the infestation of western Anatolian grapes by phylloxera), grapes and raisins continued to be an important item of export from western Anatolia.[29]

The wholesale price indexes in İzmir of the major commodities exported from western Anatolia between 1840 and the 1870s are shown in Table 5.[30] According to these, all commodities experienced sharp price rises at different periods between 1840 and 1876. The most spectacular occurred in cotton, with a 300% rise between the mid-1850s and the early 1860s. The price of valonia increased by about 100%, and opium by over 80% between the 1840s and the 1870s. Even the price of madder root went up by over 30% before it declined sharply after the 1870s, when it was displaced by synthetic dyes. Furthermore, between 1840 and 1876 the rise in the prices of Ottoman exports from western Anatolia was such that it offset the relative increase in the prices of Ottoman imports, which was also going on during these years. This favorable turn in the external terms of trade of Ottoman exports from western Anatolia provided an important incentive for the local merchants to become active in export trade.[31]

TABLE 5

Price index of Valonia, Madder, Raisins, Opium, and Cotton in İzmir, 1845–1876

	Valonia	Madder	Raisins	Opium	Cotton
1845–49	100	100	100	100	100
1850–54	119	110	116	93	118
1855–59	151	119	197	124	144
1860–64	196	126	109	136	442
1865–69	197	133	117	177	261
1870–74	187	133	120	181	194
1875–76	189	49	100	179	138

Note: (1845–1849 = 100)
Sources: See Appendix, Tables A.3–A.7.

EXPANSION OF TRADE AND PRODUCTION

The possibility of obtaining higher returns motivated the intermediaries to cooperate with the foreign merchants of İzmir and invest in export-oriented trade in western Anatolia. Some of the intermediaries, especially the Levantines, acquired land (which was plentiful) and rented it out to peasants in small plots on favorable terms and made arrangements for the cultivation of export crops. In the records of a transaction that involved the leasing of two farms by one Levantine to another that took place in İzmir in 1860, it is stated that the contract had included assurances by the lessor that the peasants who were residing on the property would cooperate with the lessee. In return, the latter had agreed to advance to the peasants one-half of their rent money.[32] While other examples of such contracts can be pointed out, overall the most important leverage the intermediaries had in their relations with the peasantry was their quasi-monopoly over credit transactions in the area. Payments for past loans could be further deferred, terms of new loans could be made more attractive, and, to a certain extent, increases in prices in İzmir could be reflected in rural prices to encourage the peasantry to produce export crops. In addition to these, the intermediaries could ensure the prompt assessment of the value of the crops for tax purposes, and payments to the peasantry for purchases in the interior could be made in a timely fashion. All these would serve to link the direct producers to the developing export network and entice them to respond to market demands. Most of these actions were carried out by the intermediaries at one time or another during the third quarter of the nineteenth century, leading to a number of developments in agriculture. The cultivation of some of the export crops, most notably grapes, increasingly concentrated in the immediate vicinity and in the suburbs of İzmir to reduce some of the transportation costs. Greeks and other non-Muslim communities who were taxed less and protected by foreign governments became prominent in farming. As with opium, those crops that could be easily cultivated in smaller plots by using family labor were given special attention. Circulation of labor increased in the area, including increased utilization of wage labor, sharecropping, tenancy, and seasonal immigration from outside western Anatolia. These developments were like threads interweaving the small peasant holdings, making it possible for increased production and exports to materialize in western Anatolia.

TABLE 6
Agricultural production and exports in İzmir, 1845–1876

| | Value of Total Agricultural Prod. in Const't 1845–49 | | Exports from İzmir | |
	Prices (in £)	Index	(Current £)	Index
1845–49	1396958	100	800000	100
1850–54	2070176	148	1373590	172
1855–59	1948724	139	2456368	307
1860–64	3307274	236	3790642	473
1865–69	3359298	240	4433030	554
1870–74	4928888	352	4247315	530
1875–76	5997022	429	4262827	533

Sources: See Appendix, Tables A.3–A.7, and, Kasaba, 1986, 375–383.

As shown in Table 6, exports increased by over five times and the volume of agricultural production by over four times in western Anatolia between 1845 and 1876.[33] During the same years, exports from the Ottoman Empire as a whole grew by about 3.5 times.[34] There are no estimates for the growth of Ottoman agricultural production for this interval.[35] A comparison of the growth of exports, however, indicates a more brisk traffic between western Anatolia and world markets than for the empire generally.

This data also allows us to estimate the total income generated by the expanding commodity production in western Anatolia in the mid-nineteenth century. For this, we have to first note that the current value of agricultural products is based mainly on the prices paid to the intermediaries in İzmir. Since these prices include the successive additions to the unit price of these commodities as they traveled from their points of production to İzmir, current value of agricultural product can be interpreted as the total income generated in agriculture in western Anatolia. As indicated in Table 7, this amount increased almost eightfold between the 1840s and the 1870s, which corresponds to approximately a sixfold increase in per capita terms. Next, we shall analyze the pattern of distribution of this newly created wealth and its effects on the various groups who participated in its generation in western Anatolia.

DISTRIBUTION OF WEALTH

Regional Disparities

Three main conduits through which wealth could be channeled out of western Anatolia were imports, taxes, and profit transfers. To take the

TABLE 7
Income generated in the agricultural sector in the Province of İzmir, 1845–1876

	Current Value of Agricultural Product (£)	Population of İzmir Province	Per Capita Income Generated in Agriculture, (£.s.)
1845–49	1396958	962428	1.9.
1850–54	2303826	1011522	2.5.
1855–59	2938596	1063120	2.15.
1860–64	7440368	1117350	6.19.
1865–69	6300940	1174346	5.7.
1870–74	7532450	1234249	6.2.
1875–76	7981834	1278007	6.5.

Note: 1% annual growth of population is assumed on the basis of Karpat 1983, 216.
Sources: Appendix, Tables A.3–A.7; Kasaba 1986, 375–383; Cuinet 1892; Karpat 1978, 258.

last first, railroads constituted the only field where there was some investment by foreign capital in western Anatolia during the mid-nineteenth century, but these ventures did not attain a comfortable level of profitability to draw large sums out of the area before the 1870s.[36] Therefore, profit transfers could not have amounted to much as a means of siphoning wealth out of the region. A close examination of imports and taxes in western Anatolia also suggests that neither of these mechanisms generated enough of a force to capture a significant part of the wealth that was created through the export trade.

First, unlike general Ottoman foreign trade, the port of İzmir consistently exported more than it imported throughout the nineteenth century, especially during the century's middle decades.[37] Therefore, even if the current account of western Anatolian or İzmir's foreign trade was cleared annually and promptly by paying for imports with the money earned from exports, there would be a substantial sum left in the area after all accounts were settled. In reality, the sum that was left in the area was even larger than that suggested by the foreign trade balance of the city, because payments for imports were always in arrears. This was owing to the lag between the time of the year when exports were brought to İzmir for shipment and that when the imports were unloaded for disbursement in the area. Also, there were persistent difficulties in generating an acceptable currency from among the different kinds of money circulating in İzmir to pay the foreign merchants for the imported merchandise. Bills of exchange were used commonly in lieu of payments, and sometimes it took years for these bills to be cleared in European markets.[38]

As for the sums that were transmitted toward the central government in taxes, these were considerable. As a prosperous region, western Anatolia was always one of the highest contributors to the government treasury. The province of İzmir alone was contributing close to 10% of both the tithe and total revenue of the Porte.[39] With the other provinces in the region, this percentage would probably come closer to 25%. However, the revenues generated in western Anatolia did not increase on a par with the rate of expansion of agricultural and commercial activity in the area. In 1872, about 37 million kuruş tithe was collected in İzmir. In 1879, the first year when tithe figures become available in a systematic manner in the Ottoman Empire, İzmir's contribution to this fund was estimated to be about the same, 34.2 million kuruş.[40] Whereas, in the years 1870–74 and 1875–76 alone the volume of agricultural production in western Anatolia had increased by about 22% (see Table 6). Furthermore, provincial contributions to the imperial tithe were estimated by the central government based on the information available during the time of the auctioning of the tithe. However, because of successive subcontracting and other complexities involved, tax farmers and the local government officials could easily get away with not transmitting the tithe and other taxes intact and use it for their own purposes in their regions.[41] Therefore, it is likely that these figures even overestimate the amount of taxes collected in western Anatolia.

Little of the wealth that was thus retained in western Anatolia found its way back to the villages in the hinterland where it was originally created. Various contemporary accounts indicate that no long-lasting improvement took place in living conditions in the interior. Only sporadically did the peasants enjoy a relative improvement in their purchasing power, depending on the willingness of the intermediaries to reflect the high prices onto their transactions in the hinterland; furthermore, this amelioration would be contingent upon the peasants' ability to hide this income from tax collectors. Such payments by the intermediaries to the producers was the only established channel through which funds could be disbursed in the countryside. There was virtually no government investment, and despite a number of fairly ambitious beginnings, foreign investment had failed to take root. Also, most of the articles imported into the port of İzmir were destined for consumption by the urban classes.[42] There was, in other words, a marked discrepancy between the large cities (especially İzmir) and the countryside in terms of how much each part contributed to agricultural production and how much it benefited from the trade that was based on this sector.

There were several reasons for the growing concentration of wealth in coastal areas, especially in İzmir. First among them was the disproportionality of the tax burden. In spite of the initial plans of the Tanzimat to achieve a more equitable distribution of taxation between the town and the country, agriculture's share of government revenues continued to increase during the third quarter of the nineteenth century. According to some calculations, in 1872–73, farmers directly contributed 45% of total government revenues in the form of tithe and animal tax, and they were also responsible for most of an additional 32%.[43] There existed similar patterns in the distribution of the tax burden in western Anatolia. At both the imperial and the provincial levels, although the farmers were directly contributing close to half of the government revenues, expenditures in the budgets of 1850, 1863–64, and 1872–73 that benefited them directly amounted to no more than 8% to 10% of total government disbursements.[44]

Second, in western Anatolia commerce-related activities were overwhelmingly centralized in the coastal areas, and especially in İzmir. Not only were services such as insurance, customs, and brokerage, stationed there, but processing of the commodities (sorting, weighing, packaging) was done around the port as well. The intermediaries who played such an important role in coordinating the flow of goods from the countryside, in tax farming, and in finance, were for the most part domiciled in the city. Consequently, as the trade of western Anatolia expanded, İzmir grew larger and became ever more important. Between the 1840s and the 1880s its population grew at more than 2% per annum, which was more than the estimated rate of demographic growth in the Ottoman Empire as a whole.[45] By the 1880s, with a population of more than 200,000, İzmir had become one of the largest cities in the Ottoman Empire. It possessed a fairly extensive network of main and side streets, some of which were built in the 1860s by a French company as a part of the quay project.[46] In the 1860s, some of these streets were lit by the gas company founded by the British.[47] Compared to what existed in other cities of the empire in urban infrastructure and services, some parts of İzmir were quite advanced and impressive. After İstanbul, it was the most cosmopolitan city of the Ottoman Empire, with Muslims composing less than one-half of the city's population. This diversity was reflected in its lively and colorful cultural life, which produced, among other things, five newspapers in different languages, seventeen printing houses, a library that filled ten houses (not counting those that were attached to various mosques), and one of the first theaters in the Ottoman Empire.[48]

With the conspicuous wealth of its rich residents and their lifestyles, İzmir was becoming a booming metropole, its development far exceeding not only the western Anatolian countryside but also that of the other cities in the region. In the 1880s, when İzmir's population had passed 200,000, it had become six times the size of Aydın, the second largest city of the province. But the main influx of people into İzmir was not from its hinterland but from the Balkans, the Archipelago, and from other parts of the empire. These were people who were ejected from their homes for a number of economic or political reasons and who were either settled by the Ottoman government or were attracted by İzmir's flourishing economy.[49] In other words, it would be wrong to view the growth of İzmir in the second half of the nineteenth century as an aspect of a broad process or urbanization in western Anatolia. It should be remembered that in those years, over 70% of the people in the province were still living in rural areas.[50] Many reports of persisting rural misery suggest that the marketing network that connected İzmir to its hinterland served to accentuate the sharp distinction between "city" and "countryside" that had been embedded in the classical system. But it would be equally wrong to conclude that the patterns of relationship between town and countryside had remained the same since the classical period. For one thing, the division of labor that defined the respective positions of these social spaces had changed in important ways. Now, their respective places were defined, not according to their position within the redistributive system, but according to their relationship to the global division of labor.[51] Old centers that had served as relay points of the redistributive system were either like Salonika, changing into, or like Aydın, being replaced by, entrepôts of trade that linked the various parts of the Ottoman Empire to other areas of the capitalist world economy.[52]

Social Hierarchies

During the middle decades of the nineteenth century, the expansion of export trade in western Anatolia benefited four groups in varying degrees. The peasant households who were located in the immediate vicinity of coastal towns were able to organize the production and transportation of their crops without being dependent on third parties. By doing so, they took advantage of the favorable conditions in the export markets in western Anatolia.[53] As for those that were located in the interior, macro evidence we have presented suggests little, if any, improvement in their overall conditions during the century. Nevertheless, since the transmission of price increases into the countryside was one of the ways in which the intermediaries were able to persuade the farmers to produce certain crops, the prosperous conditions of the mid-nineteenth century must have had a positive impact even on some of those dispersed units in the countryside, at least intermittently.[54]

The nomadic tribes who owned and operated camel caravans in western Anatolia also benefited from the expansion of production and exports. At the initial stages of the boom, rail had not yet displaced the earlier forms of transportation. Even in those places touched by the railroad, camel caravans were still the most efficient means of bringing the produce to the terminals; and in the rest of the region, they were to remain the only means of transportation for a long time. In 1866, almost half the traffic between İzmir and Aydın was carried by camels.[55] As late as 1872, there were still ten thousand camels in western Anatolia which constituted one-fifth of camels in all of Anatolia.[56]

Camels and caravans were owned and operated by nomadic tribes. Since they were not engaged in sedentary agriculture, these tribes did not pay the tithe, and were, in fact, one of the least taxed groups within the empire. The indispensable service they provided afforded them an autonomy they fought to preserve whenever it was threatened.[57] Camel-rearing tribes benefited from all kinds of traffic in the area whether during times of mobilization for war (as during the Crimean War) or during the expansion of trade (as in the mid-1860s).[58]

The third group who saw an increase in their income during the mid-nineteenth century were those who were part- or full-time wage workers in the cities and in the countryside. Money wages in the Ottoman Empire increased by about 60% between the periods 1839–49 and 1870–79—a growth that was especially intense during the Crimean War, the cotton boom, and in the first half of the 1870s.[59] As show in Table 8, wages in western Anatolia followed a similar trend, registering significant increase during these periods of expanded commercial activity. In absolute terms, urban wages for skilled workers (masons, carpenters, etc.) were greater than wages paid for agricultural workers; on the other hand, unskilled workers in cities were earning as much as their counterparts employed in agriculture. Also, generally, the wages in the two settings were moving together. Even though during the second half of the nineteenth century imported manufactures started to invade Ottoman markets, presumably displacing many peasants from traditional manufacturing activities, there does not seem to have been an influx of people into the cities to pressure urban wages downward. This suggests that

TABLE 8
Wages in Western Anatolia (kuruş/day)

| | Nonagricultural | | Agricultural | |
	Skilled	Unskilled	General	Source
Bursa				
1851			6	FO 78/905: 69
1854		4.5		Issawi 1980, 40
1855	22	8.3		FO 78/1111: 44–50
				FO 78/1209: 60–80
1856	15	9	10.5	FO 78/1302: 338–57
				Issawi 1980, 40
1858			7.5	FO 78/1450: 72
1859			14.5	FO 78/1534: 30–39
1860		8	8.5	FO 78/1609: 36, 69
1862	10.5		9.25	FO 78/1771: 57
1864	11		9.75	FO 78/1876: 48
1865	11		6.5	Issawi 1980, 42
İzmir				
1841	12.5			Issawi 1980, 40
1842	12			Issawi 1980, 40
1856			5.5	Issawi 1980, 40
1863			9.5	Issawi 1980, 41
1870			8.7	Issawi 1980, 42
1872	15–20			Scherzer 1873, 25

displaced peasants or those who were seeking to supplement their incomes usually remained in the countryside and sought and found employment as wageworkers, sharecroppers, or tenant farmers.[60] Furthermore, between 1841 and 1864, when the prices of subsistence and consumption items doubled, wages went up by about three times. In other words, wage workers in western Anatolia had not only a nominal but also a real improvement in their earnings.[61]

The group who benefited most from the export boom of the mid-nineteenth century were the non-Muslim intermediaries who had captured the strategic positions of the commercial network in western Anatolia at the end of the eighteenth century.[62] Under the prosperous conditions of the mid-nineteenth century, non-Muslim intermediaries, while limiting foreigners' access to the region, magnified and multiplied their own connections in and out of western Anatolia. They exploited their informal links with their coreligionists who had emigrated to Europe and America, and in some instances they improved their existing connections into large networks of trading companies with branch offices in Europe, America, and Russia as well as in the Ottoman Empire.[63]

At the same time, intermediaries benefited from the Tanzimat legislation that eased their tax burden, introduced security of property, and made it easier for them to acquire, transfer, and inherit property. And finally, there was the eagerness with which foreign governments, as part of their interstate policies, pursued the issue of protecting the rights of the non-Muslim communities in the Ottoman Empire.

One way we can gauge the extent to which non-Muslims used the mid-nineteenth century boom to their advantage is through an examination of their accumulated property. According to the wills that were deposited with the British consular court and with the Ottoman courts in İzmir, by far the wealthiest estates belonged to non-Muslims. Some of these were valued at more than 500,000 kuruş.[64] In addition to jewelry, chinaware, and cash, all of them had acquired extensive tracts of land, houses, warehouses, and stores. Depositions show that some of them possessed as many as five stores.[65] Their houses were large, with two floors—which was a sign of affluence at the time—and five or more rooms. Some of these houses were valued from 25,000 to 110,000 kuruş.[66] To appreciate the relative standing of the holders of these properties, we should compare their worth with the following figures: The salary of the British Consul in İzmir was about 20,000 kuruş per year;[67] the governor of Bursa, one of the highest paid officials, was receiving 200,000 kuruş per year;[68] in 1871, the famous author Ahmet Mithat Efendi signed with the newspaper *Basiret* for a monthly salary of 1,000 kr;[69] and the daily wage of a skilled worker in İzmir was fifteen kuruş a day, which, in three hundred days a year, amounted to an annual income of 4,500 kuruş.

Some groups in the non-Muslim community took more advantage of the favorable circumstances. In the empire as a whole, Armenians and Greeks were far ahead of other non-Muslim communities. Armenian influence rose largely out of their banking operations in İstanbul and in other major cities of the empire. Their strength in this field was not limited to private companies but included as well some prestigious positions in the bureaucracy. For example, the three most important posts in the imperial mint were occupied by Armenians during most of the nineteenth century, and one of these, the superintendent, came from the same Armenian family (Düzians) almost without interruption between 1757 and 1880.[70] Greeks owed their position in part to the strength of their organization within the hierarchy of the Orthodox church, as this was recognized by the Ottoman government.[71] But more important was their concentration in some of the wealthiest parts of the Ottoman Empire, such as the Balkans and western Anatolia. In these regions they became the perennial merchants of both the intraregional and export trade. Naturally, in areas of high concentration of non-Muslim populations like western Anatolia, there were Greeks, Armenians, and Jews in different occupations with different levels of wealth and prestige. Nevertheless, the overall standing of non-Muslims in the social hierarchy of the Ottoman Empire in the nineteenth century was Levantines first, then Greeks, Armenians, and Jews, in that order. The relative standings of these groups was also reflected in the differences between their neighborhoods in İzmir, where the most prosperous quarters were located in the north and in the suburbs, and were occupied by foreigners and Levantines. As one moved southward through the Greek, Armenian, and Jewish quarters, the neighborhoods became increasingly poorer and more congested.[72]

The rise of non-Muslim merchants to wealth and prominence in western Anatolia took place largely at the expense of the predominantly Muslim elite. First among them were the merchants of the classical era, who had accumulated impressive fortunes in the transit, local, and intraregional trade.[73] The second group was the provincial representatives of the government bureaucracy. The third group were the ayans of the late eighteenth century who had acquired local power through extending their *iltizam* holdings and raising private armies. Except for the ayan, the fortunes of the Muslim potentates generally rose in tandem with the fortunes of the central government. Their positions were defined within the parameters of the classical system, and their power tended to depend on the effectiveness of the power and authority of the Porte. With the incorporation of the Ottoman Empire into the world economy, nonmarket processes, which had been the main ligaments of the classical system, were subsumed by the processes of the capitalist world system. This meant that the conditions of existence of these Muslim potentates were to a large extent undermined.

Muslim merchants were relegated to a secondary position by the changing of the trade routes. Not only were they not as familiar with the European markets as were the non-Muslim merchants, but they were also deprived of the lucrative routes and markets that had been guaranteed by the central government since the classical period. By the nineteenth century, the tax liabilities of the Muslim and non-Muslim merchants were also reversed. In the classical period, Muslim merchants were granted various tax exemptions, but in the nineteenth century, according to one count, they were burdened with eighty *şer'i* and ninety-seven *örfi* taxes, while the liabilities of the non-Muslim merchants were being simplified and externally guaranteed.[74] As Muslim merchants lost the pivotal role they once played in the regional and foreign trade of the empire, they increasingly became dependent on non-Muslim merchants and bankers for imports and for obtaining loans.[75]

The position of provincial administrators was somewhat more complex. The declining power of the central government gave them the liberty to use or abuse their power. Frequently they tried to supplement their incomes by restricting the market processes, imposing illegal dues, and instituting purchasing monopolies.[76] However, the decline of the Porte's power had deprived provincial administrators of security in tenure and, more important, from any substantive link with their place of office. Not holding any timars, they had no more responsibility for or to their provincial lands and people. Increasingly, they became an idle class, living off the rent. None of their attempts to restrict the market processes was effective in the long run because they invariably met with protests and rejection by the better-connected and more powerful groups of the province. Nevertheless, in the short run, they were sometimes disruptive enough to cause fluctuations in the volume of foreign trade, especially in the early years of the nineteenth century.[77] As the century proceeded, the helplessness of local officials became more and more apparent, making them ever more imprudent in their exploitation of local resources and in the execution of their administrative duties.

Ayans were different from the merchants and administrators in that they were the products not of the classical period but of the period of incorporation. Their rise to power was originally related more to the weakening than to the strength of the Porte. Nevertheless, even at their peak at the turn of the nineteenth century, they never had anything but a distant relationship with the land and the people. This relationship consisted of leasing, subcontracting, and sharecropping arrangements that were mediated to a large extent by the non-Muslim sarrafs. For the ayans of Anatolia, especially, their nominal association with the Porte increasingly became more important in perpetuating their power in their localities than any other affiliation they might have had locally. Around İzmir, the two most influential families were the Araboğlus and the Karaosmanoğlus who, according to the French consul in the late eighteenth century, were among the "richest persons in the Ottoman Empire."[78] The same source indicates that "even though these families had accumulated wealth from cotton and wheat," neither of them had a "feudal or manorial type relationship on their lands," and, "no mention is made of either family as either producers or furnishers of French trade in the area. . . ."[79] Seventy years later the Karaosmanoğlu family was still in place in western Anatolia, and neither their relations with the landholding peasantry nor the substance of their power had changed much. In 1845, one of its members was the governor and according to the British consul, "half the town of Manisa and many villages belong[ed] to the family." Then, the governor made sure that "the town of Manisa and environs [were] taxed moderately because he [did] not want to burden his relations' property too heavily."[80] As the nineteenth century progressed, the ayan became ever more distant from their rural properties. As with the muslim merchants and the governors, they too were becoming increasingly dependent on non-Muslim sarrafs in Istanbul and in western Anatolia to maintain their tax farms and their status in the area; and, as their debts accumulated, they started to lose title to their properties as well.[81] Especially after the land code of 1858, along with peasants, local ayans were selling their properties, and almost all the buyers were non-Muslims.[82]

One other factor that undermined the position of Muslims in land-related matters was the strict application of the Koranic Law. When the Sharia Courts apportioned the estates of the deceased owners, larger holdings would be divided into small pieces. It was also common for Muslim families to designate large pieces of urban and rural property as waqf. This arrangement both limited the taxability of such properties and, depending on the type of waqf, rendered them unproductive for generations to come.[83] The records show that when the properties of non-Muslims were divided up by the Ottoman courts the heirs would buy each other's shares and thereby preserve the integrity of their holdings and sometimes even expand their size, although this was not a common practice among Muslims.[84]

While the changes that were related to agriculture, trade, banking, and administration undermined the social status of the Muslim elite, certain developments in the manufacturing sector adversely affected other segments of this community. Historically, Muslims were more identified with crafts such as tanning, saddling, shoe making, wool and silk weaving, and dyeing; Armenians worked more as tinsmiths, locksmiths, silversmiths, goldsmiths, and construction workers. The specializations of Greeks included bricklaying, winemaking, cobbling, and small shopkeeping. Aside from the few and isolated examples of bankers and traders, Jews of western Anatolia were predominantly occupied as itinerant workers or traveling merchants during the middle decades of the nineteenth century.[85] While the viability of most of these crafts were adversely affected by inexpensive European imports, textile-related occupations—where Muslims were especially well-represented—faced particularly fierce competition and declined rapidly after the middle decades of the nineteenth century.[86]

CONCLUSION

By the 1840s the classical system of production and distribution had been replaced by a new social matrix in western Anatolia. A group of mostly non-Muslim "banker cum merchants" were entrenched in the controlling positions of this matrix. This group derived its power from having access to liquidity. In western Anatolia, the mid-nineteenth century boom occurred according to the terms set by these intermediaries, who also succeeded in appropriating most of the wealth that grew out of this boom.

One outcome of this configuration was the strengthening of the peripheral networks that had been supporting the social status of the intermediaries since the end of the eighteenth century. This meant that the links between the Ottoman Empire and the world economy would continue to be reproduced in a manner that was devoid of any long-term organizational or structural stability. In specific terms, rather than acquiring a long-term competitive strength in the world economy, processes of production in the Ottoman Empire would become significant only conjuncturally, under exceptional circumstances. Spatially, the newly created wealth concentrated in commercial centers on the coast; socially, non-Muslim bankers, merchants, usurers, and tax farmers multiplied their riches and influence at the expense of the various segments of the Muslim community who were associated with the classical system either in its pure or its distorted form.

What must be emphasized is that both the distribution of wealth along these lines and the transmission of the increased European demand and prices into western Anatolia took place primarily within the framework of market relations. Some groups, like the conservative bureaucrats in Istanbul and provincial officials, tried to intervene and alter these processes in an effort to revive the classical power relations. Others, such as the foreigners and the Tanzimat bureaucrats, tried to influence the same processes by strengthening the political structures and institutions of the empire. The failure of both of these groups underscores the unique importance of the mid-nineteenth century as the only era in which market exchange set effective limits to the efficacy of political forms of (re)organization and domination in western Anatolia and in the Ottoman Empire in general. In the end, it was the market processes that permeated and integrated western Anatolian social structures as a peripheral region of the capitalist world economy.

5

The Great Depression and Beyond

THE YEAR BETWEEN the 1870s and 1890s (most commonly, 1873–96) are generally referred to as "the great depression of the nineteenth century" in the annals of European economic history. What set this period off as one of contraction was the deflationary trend that affected the prices of all the principal articles of commerce in the world economy.[1] The general decline in prices progressed faster than the decline in nominal wages, especially in the core areas.[2] This squeezed the profitability of industrial production in core and semiperipheral zones of the capitalist world economy and disrupted the arteries of commerce that had been established during the preceding era. The stronger states protected their markets and the profitability of their industries by erecting high tariff barriers. This led to the gradual emergence of some of the semiperipheral areas of the previous era (most notably Germany and the United States) as new loci of accumulation, providing the ground for their subsequent challenge of British hegemony in world markets.[3] One of the consequences of the widespread practice of protectionism was the fracturing of the world market. This in turn made it difficult for the investors and financial houses to find new conduits for their accumulated funds. Finance capital (or *haute finance* in Polanyi's terms), which grew out of the ensemble of these two elements, became increasingly channeled toward speculative ventures, both exploiting and exacerbating the unpredictable conditions that were created by the divided world economy.[4]

107

The speculative mania that was followed by the panic and the "crash" of the 1890s, however, forced the captains of finance capital to seek closer cooperation with the core and semiperipheral states.[5] In this way, capital, which had been accumulated through supranational means, was becoming a vehicle for the competition of core and semiperipheral states in the world economic and political arena. That part of capital that was generated in the new loci of production like Germany, had been in symbiosis with state structures from the very beginning. Hence, in these instances, the expansion of "national" capital was closely related to the policies enacted by these states.[6]

From the collusion between finance capital and state structures, on the one hand, and from the development of national industries in Europe, on the other, was born the imperialist policies of expansion, where several states of Europe undertook to find and protect new markets and sources of raw materials for their growing industries and/or areas of investment for the accumulated capital. The concomitant expansion of core and semiperipheral states in competition with each other created the means for the diversion of accumulated funds from speculation toward investment in productive ventures beyond Europe. In this way, imperialist policies of the late nineteenth century became one of the principal forces that helped move the world economy out of the slump and into a new era of expansion in the 1890s.

The new configuration of forces that grew out of the downturn of the last quarter of the nineteenth century involved the replacement of British hegemony by a rivalry among several core and semiperipheral states for establishing and enlarging their respective spheres of domination in the world economy. Compared with the first three quarters, the last quarter of the nineteenth century was inherently unstable.[7] Initially, peripheral areas served as the main theater where the core states and bourgeoisies competed with each other; but as the intensity of this competition increased, the tensions reflected back on the continent. Eventually, the tendency toward conflict prevailed over the countervailing forces in Europe and paved the way toward the Great War of the early twentieth century.

What effect did these new developments have on the Ottoman Empire? During the thirty-two years between 1876 and 1908, the Empire was ruled by the same monarch, Abdülhamid II. While the rule of his predecessors was characterized by an indecisive coalescence of conflicting tendencies on the level of the Ottoman state, Abdülhamid's reign is generally recognized as one in which political power was recentralized in the hands of a narrow circle of officials who were closely affiliated with the Palace. This represented a significant shift from the Tanzimat era, when the Porte (i.e., the government) had acquired substantial power.[8] Under Abdülhamid, a narrowly defined bureaucracy which was intolerant of opposition and obsessed with security moved the Empire further away from the Tanzimat era. The canons of early republican historiography blamed the inhibition of progress that had been initiated during the middle decades of the nineteenth century primarily on the Hamidian regime.

However, as research has progressed, these notions about the late nineteenth century Ottoman Empire have been refined and recently completely revised. The new appreciation of Abdülhamid and his rule is mostly based on some or all of the following findings: first, there was a significant rise in government revenues during the last quarter of the nineteenth century;[9] second, as implemented by Abdülhamid, administrative centralization contributed to this growth, ended the uncertain waverings of government policies, and strengthened the Ottoman state vis-à-vis both external and internal forces and groups;[10] third, the educational reform that Abdülhamid's administration achieved, undermined the assertions about the conservativism of his rule;[11] fourth, the Ottoman economy in general,[12] and Ottoman agriculture in particular,[13] grew at moderate if not impressive rates during these years, owing mainly to the strengthening of the Ottoman state and to the austere policies pursued by the Ottoman government; finally, the Ottoman state managed to pay back substantial parts of the previous loans, which is taken to be a further indicator of the success of the economic policies pursued during these years.

While the research that led to these findings is extremely useful and impressive, some of the revisionist interpretation that flowed out of them has proven to be even more problematic than the previous appraisals of the last years of the Ottoman Empire. First, the political survival of the Ottoman state through the latter part of the nineteenth century should be attributed to the nature and acuteness of interstate rivalry in the world economy rather than to any policy that may have been initiated by Abdülhamid and his governments. After Britain refocused its Near Eastern strategy toward Cyprus and Egypt, none of the other competing powers was strong enough to absorb the Ottoman Empire alone. For the second time in the nineteenth century, the empire was located in the interstices of hegemonic rivalry,[14] where it survived for almost another fifty years as a formally independent entity. Absence of direct administrative control by any one European power allowed Ottoman officialdom latitude in taking different sides in the different conflicts that took place among core and semiperipheral states in the late nineteenth and early twentieth centuries. These conditions also allowed some room for the development of two social movements, that of the Young Turks and that of Mustafa Kemal, that were manifestly bent on gaining control of the Ottoman state apparatus.

However, the formal nature of this independence should be underscored. During the last decades of the nineteenth century, supranational finance capital acquired direct control over Ottoman finances and over some of the more important activities of production in the Ottoman Empire through the Public Debt Administration (PDA) and its affiliated organizations.[15] Therefore, even though it was formally independent, the ability of the Ottoman government to articulate and implement its policies was substantively curtailed. The PDA consisted of a seven-man council representing the creditors of the Ottoman state, to which a huge bureaucracy of permanent administrators was attached. Its main purpose was to generate sufficient funds to meet the interest and some of the principal on the empire's external debt by administering the revenue sources that were ceded to it by the Ottoman government. These sources included the salt monopoly, the stamp tax, the spirits due, the fish tax, the silk tithe, the annual tribute from several provinces, and the tobacco tax, which the PDA administered through a special agency called Régie des Tabac.[16] Between its establishment in 1881 and the First World War, the PDA controlled from one-quarter to one-third of the revenues of the government,[17] and by 1907, debt services had reached to absorb 30% of the export earnings of the Ottoman Empire.[18]

This background makes it clear that the Ottoman government of the late nineteenth century was closely restrained in its options to improve revenue generation or administrative efficiency independently of the PDA. The empire's best and most fruitful resources were pledged to this agency, and the capitulations that were still in effect prevented the government from adjusting any of its remaining sources of income.[19]

PDA was not under the influence or direction of any one power. All major European states were represented in its administrative council, and the respective governments had considerable input in the selection of the delegates to that body. Thus, as an institution, the PDA embodied the dual relationship between governments and supranational capital. It served the combined interests of the rival powers that had converged on maintaining the Ottoman Empire and securing the funds that had been invested there.[20] These aims were quite close to those the British had pursued during the middle decades of the nineteenth century; but unlike the British, supranational finance capital was successful in propping up the Ottoman state. The presence of the PDA brought fiscal stability to the Empire, improved its credit worthiness in Europe; and the well-oiled bureaucracy of the PDA was one of the main forces behind improved tithe revenues in the late nineteenth century.[21]

The organization of the PDA grew quickly. Shortly after its establishment it had 3,040 full-time employees; in 1915, this number had gone up to 5,278.[22] As aided by the older and the newer banks, its administrative offshoots and the monopolies it was administering, the PDA's influence expanded beyond the Ottoman state and covered almost the entire empire.[23] The entrenchment of finance capital in the Ottoman Empire in a well-organized and coordinated manner through the PDA effectively displaced the intermediaries from their strategic positions in most of the Anatolian countryside.[24] Here then was another field where finance capital was immensely more successful than the British, who had repeatedly tried but failed to uproot the local intermediaries from the commercial networks in western Anatolia.[25] The intermediaries witnessed the curtailment of their access to the traditional fields of money lending and arbitrage, and also lost the marketing opportunities they had seized during the middle decades of the nineteenth century. After the 1880s, the external terms of trade turned against Ottoman exports, once again rendering foreign trade a risky and unprofitable activity for local merchants.[26] In other words, during the great depression of the nineteenth century the intermediaries lost the uniquely advantageous position that had allowed them to control the overall rhythm of economic activity in their regions. The forceful entry of the PDA and particularly that of the Régie into the Ottoman agriculture provoked widespread resentment and protests in various parts of Anatolia. Tobacco producers, especially, in collaboration with local merchants, resorted to smuggling their produce out of the empire to circumvent the powerful enforcement agency the Régie had set up. In the short term, these tactics created significant disruption in the Régie's activities,[27] but in the long run they were not strong enough to permanently reverse the PDA's presence in the Anatolian countryside.

The relative stabilization of Ottoman finances and the displacement of local intermediaries were significant developments, but neither of them affected the status of the Ottoman Empire in the division of labor of the capitalist world economy. Other than the addition of tobacco to the list of major exports[28] (which was in the hands of the Régie) and the Ottoman Empire becoming a net importer of grains,[29] there was no significant change in the type of commodities the empire exchanged in the world markets from the mid- to late nineteenth century.[30] The pattern of land distribution remained similar to that in the mid-nineteenth century, where the majority of production units still consisted of small peasant holdings.[31] During the great depression of the nineteenth century, the Ottoman Empire, along with other peripheral areas, contributed to the accumulation of finance capital at its supranational level through profit transfers and debt repayments.[32] After the turn of the twentieth century, when world market conditions improved, the Ottoman Empire still had a relatively open economy with a large foreign trade sector.[33]

The reassertion of bureaucratic centralism under the aegis of the supranational finance capital had little effect on the position of the Ottoman Empire in the world economy, but it was significant in altering local power relations. The undermining of the status of the intermediaries meant that non-Muslims were excluded from the hub of economic activity. Thus, at the turn of the twentieth century, when Ottoman exports picked up again, the state bureaucracy and the new Muslim bourgeoisie, which it was actively promoting, became the main beneficiaries of this new boom.[34] The relative isolation of the non-Muslims during the late nineteenth century was also significant politically in that it created the ground for the successful implementation of policies of national enclosure between 1908 and 1923.

6

Conclusion

Most of the treatises on the Turkish Republic start by pointing out the legacy of the Ottoman past. Most commonly, this refers to the hypertrophied presence of the Turkish state within Turkish society. One of the main conclusions of this study is that it is erroneous to posit a direct and continuous line of inheritance between the Ottoman Empire and the Turkish Republic in this respect, because the two entities were substantively different. While as a world empire, the centrality of the imperial apparatus was integral to the empire, the bureaucratic centralism of the republic grew out of a particular phase in the development of the capitalist world economy during the last quarter of the nineteenth century. It is not even entirely appropriate to talk about the Ottoman state within the context of the classical empire, where such an entity could not be separated from the imperial totality. The Ottoman state, as distinct from the Ottoman Empire, should be seen as a product of the transformations that entailed the incorporation and peripheralization of the Ottoman Empire within the context of the capitalist world economy.

Second, the classical empire and the restructured peripheral entity that became the Turkish Republic were separated by a crucial interval in the nineteenth century when market exchange and political domination had become alternative forms of integrating the Ottoman social structures. As late as the middle of the nineteenth century, neither the

113

bureaucratic centralism nor peripherality of the Ottoman Empire/Turkey were foregone conclusions. Primarily, it was local intermediaries who shaped the content and direction of social change in the Ottoman Empire toward peripheralization. They managed to selectively thwart Tanzimat policies, the regional designs of the British government, and the attempted incursions by the British and other foreign capital into the Ottoman Empire, especially during the 1840s and 1850s. In short, it was their activities that strengthened market exchange rather than political domination as the pivotal axis of integration in the dissolving empire. One of the key points that needs to be emphasized is that the intermediaries were firmly entrenched in local networks in the aftermath of the Napoleonic Wars when a vacuum was created in Near Eastern trade following the withdrawal of the French. The nature of this conjuncture is significant because it highlights the importance of local relations for the rise of this class, as opposed to the more common perceptions, which tend to see them as mere offshoots of foreign interests and capital in the Ottoman Empire. By the 1850s, the intermediaries were rooted in the local networks so firmly that when world market conditions improved for Ottoman products, they were able to exploit these favorable conditions for their own benefit and to the exclusion of foreign and domestic competitors. In subsequent years, foreigners and the local intermediaries often found themselves in competition more than in cooperation with each other. By looking at the type of inter-relatedness that was sustained between western Anatolia and the core areas of the capitalist world economy, and at the effect of the growth in production and trade on the region, we concluded that the development of the Ottoman Empire during the middle decades of the nineteenth century was peripheral in character and that non-Muslim intermediaries were the main brokers and beneficiaries of the peripheralization of the Ottoman Empire. But the historical antagonism between the non-Muslim intermediaries and foreign capital and capitalists suggests that the commonly held inferences about the compradore nature of the former are misleading for this period.[1] It is more appropriate to view the local intermediaries as capitalists who were bent on maximizing their returns. Under the conditions of the mid-nineteenth century, their short-term interests were linked to the peripheralization of the Ottoman Empire, even if this put them in opposition to the policies of the hegemonic power of the capitalist world economy.

Third, after the 1870s, these peripheral networks that had developed earlier in the nineteenth century were taken over by the Ottoman bureaucracy, which was in cooperation with the supranational finance capital. This led to the economic (and subsequently political) isolation of the non-Muslims intermediaries in the social matrixes of the empire. If examined retrospectively, this development can be seen as the main factor that stifled the further expansion of the social space within which the power of the intermediaries was rooted. Had it continued to grow unchecked, this space could have become germane to the development of a genuine civil society within the disintegrating empire. Thus, far from being the legacy of the Ottoman system, bureaucratic centralism of the late nineteenth and early twentieth centuries was imposed and instituted under the auspices of core capital and core states of the capitalist world economy. Concomitantly, the weakness of civil society in the later years of the empire and in the early years of the republic grew out of a particular conjuncture in the development of the capitalist world economy rather than being the descendant of the Near Eastern culture that had been embedded in the classical institutions of the Ottoman Empire.

This work is equally contentious in its rejection of the claim that the dissolution of the Ottoman Empire consisted of one long decline that started with the first contacts with the European economy. To begin with, there was at least one interval during the first half of the eighteenth century when the economic and political processes in the Ottoman Empire seemed to take an upward turn. We have also demonstrated that the peripheralization of the Ottoman Empire proceeded through at least two major turning points. The first of these fell around the 1800s, when the field of attraction for Ottoman territories shifted from the continent to Britain. After France had withdrawn from the eastern Mediterranean and before Britain became the dominant power in the area, there occurred a hiatus in the Empire's relations with the world economy. Tendencies toward the development of large-scale estate agriculture in the Ottoman Empire dissipated during this brief interval. The second turning point took place around the 1870s. Then, as an integrative process, market exchange was prevented from developing further by a weak (albeit recentralized) bureaucracy that was propped up by the supranational finance capital. The first transformation underlay the specialization of Ottoman territories in the production of agricultural and raw materials, where the typical unit of production was a small peasant holding and where the Empire possessed no competitive strength in any one commodity in the world markets. The transformations that occurred in the 1870s involved the institutionalization of the Ottoman state as an apparatus that was weak both in terms of not having any substantive link with the sites of production, producers, merchants, or bankers, and in terms of its subjugation to the loci of power in the core areas of the world economy. The first turning point involved the concretization of the foundation upon which the peripheral sites of production were built and around which the networks of circulation were woven; the second involved the tapping of this grid by a peripheral state. As for the economic growth that occurred in between, this served, above all, to reinforce the underlying peripheral networks.

These turning points are significant not only for having generated the two basic characteristics of the Ottoman Empire/Turkey as a peripheral social structure, but also for being located in two intervals where historical alternatives to the peripheralization of the Ottoman Empire had converged.[2] Around the 1800s there was the possibility of the strengthening of the Ottoman state with support from Britain that, had it materialized, could have created the conditions for the semiperipheralization of the Ottoman Empire/Turkey. This route was blocked by local intermediaries. On the other hand, the 1870s could have ushered a new era in which the intermediaries who had accumulated considerable wealth could invest their funds in productive ventures, expand their power bases, and develop new means of wielding state power. The organized and institutionalized penetration of supranational finance capital into the Anatolian countryside removed this alternative from the realm of possibilities for the Ottoman Empire.

The dual significance of these turning points portends the futility of ascribing a simple direction (incline or decline) or a predestined pathway to social change within the capitalist world economy. Peripheralization of the Ottoman Empire was an outcome of a broad historical transformation that, following incorporation, proceeded through various points such as these where several groups with conflicting interests stood in relation with each other. Some of these groups were the products of the developing relations with the world economy; others were descendants of an old order and were trying to hold onto their obsolete connections to perpetuate their status and power. The social environment within which these groups interacted was ultimately conditioned by the particular phase and stage of the development of the capitalist world economy, but at the same time, the outcome of their interaction was one of the constitutive elements of these same phases and stages. It is only within the context of an analysis that takes into account the complexity of both sides of this relationship as well as its two-way nature that we can adequately understand the nature of the long road that moved the Ottoman world empire to the status of a peripheral structure in the capitalist world economy.

Appendix

The following figures are derived from unpublished sources for 1840–60, and from published official and private sources for the period after 1860. While the lists are fairly complete, the reader should be aware of their limitations while interpreting them. The nineteenth-century statistics about the Ottoman Empire abound in inconsistencies in units and methods of measurement. For example, a unit of weight such as the okka had different values in different regions, as well as in different localities within a region. It also varied according to the merchandise that was being weighed. Furthermore, certain goods such as wheat and opium had their own units of measurement that were not used in weighing other goods.[1] The complexity of Ottoman metrology becomes even more apparent if we take into consideration that these units were modified, completely abandoned, or replaced by others in the course of the nineteenth century. To make matters worse, sometimes the goods were traded in units that had no consistent meaning, such as "packages," "boxes," "cases," "bundles," "baskets," etc., which then had to be weighed by government officials in public markets by weights that did not have uniform values. Even a unit such as bales, which was in widespread use in the cotton trade throughout the nineteenth century,

117

varies from 300 to 500 pounds in different sources.[2] For the classical period of the Ottoman Empire, existence of a multitude of units of measurement would not necessarily imply chaos in administration. On the contrary, this would be in conformity with general Ottoman practice of keeping many of the preconquest customs and laws, especially in the peripheral provinces of the empire, and gradually coordinating them with imperial laws. But in the nineteenth century, this situation reflected the increasing weakness of the central bureaucracy, which was unable to maintain a rigorous system of inspection to ensure the consistency of weights and measures on the local level and their coordination with those used in the center. In the same vein, the Ottoman bureaucracy failed to implement the various plans of reforming the Ottoman system of measurements that were drafted in 1640, the 1770s, 1871, 1874, 1881, and 1886.[3] We should also note that throughout the seventeenth, eighteenth, and nineteenth centuries, producers, traders, and the government officials continuously used the uncertainties of measures to their own advantage in their dealings with each other.[4]

Furthermore, there is the problem of monetary inconsistencies. One is never sure if silver, gold, or paper currency is used in determining the nominal price of an item. This needs to be known to express Ottoman prices in European currencies, because a piastre (or a kuruş) corresponded to different real values depending on the type of currency in which it was measured. These inherent incongruities of the systems of measurement render cross-regional and cross-temporal price studies and commodity aggregations extremely tentative.

In addition to these problems, one needs to mention the real source of these figures and the manner in which they were originally collected. For the most part, the following tables are drawn from the various correspondence of the British consuls in western Anatolia. The Consuls in turn used lower-ranking Ottoman officials and local merchants to collect information. Even though the consular staff usually included people who had been in their posts for a long time, it would not be realistic to expect their network of information to be sufficiently well entrenched to provide thoroughly accurate and dependable data.

It is important that we should be aware of these problems undermining the reliability of numerical representations about nineteenth-century Ottoman Empire. Ignoring them may lead to erroneous assumptions about the validity and applicability of more recent relations and concepts in earlier and different social contexts. However, it would be equally unproductive to let these limitations inhibit any research into the economic developments of an important era like the nineteenth century.

It should also be remembered that in an area that is undergoing incorporation and peripheralization, it is usual to observe archaic systems of measurement side by side with their newer and globally more meaningful counterparts. A complete standardization of weights, measures, and monies would in itself be indicative of total integration into the global division of labor.[5] We know that the incorporation of the Ottoman Empire into the capitalist world economy proceeded in parts and that throughout this long period the Ottoman political apparatus maintained its formal independence. This crucial factor contributed to the longevity of some of the Ottoman institutions and practices.

Given all these limitations, the reader should interpret both the current prices and the indexes drawn from them as approximations. To alleviate some of the short-term inconsistencies and problems, I have based most of my discussion on trends rather than absolute quantities. Also, whenever possible, I have compared the prices cited in British sources with other available information to affirm and enhance the reliability of the British data and to fill in some of the gaps that existed there.[6]

TABLE A.1
Trade of İzmir (Current Pound Sterlings) (1839–1912)

Year	Exports	Imports
1839	1,434,240	681,160
1840	—	—
1841	1,242,880	722,280
1842	1,323,400	734,000
1843	1,298,280	1,103,600
1844	—	—
1845	—	—
1846	800,000	500,000
1847	—	—
1848	—	—
1849	—	—
1850	1,449,080	1,241,240
1851	1,467,280	1,138,920
1852	1,458,000	1,140,000
1853	—	—
1854	1,120,000	1,200,000
1855	2,520,000	2,280,000
1856	2,888,840	2,874,280
1857	2,517,400	2,447,480
1858	2,230,920	2,367,280
1859	2,124,680	2,227,600
1860	1,846,360	2,386,520
1861	—	—
1862	4,518,680	2,726,320
1863	4,955,240	3,738,520
1864	3,842,286	2,538,200
1865	5,130,760	1,869,826
1866	4,156,480	2,210,988
1867	4,011,850	2,129,774
1868	—	—
1869	—	—
1870	—	—
1871	4,024,400	—
1872	4,866,840	3,473,840
1873	4,158,860	4,668,400
1874	3,939,560	4,495,300
1875	3,896,063	3,483,404
1876	4,629,590	2,859,934
1877	4,687,491	3,082,400
1878	3,542,944	4,139,907
1879	4,406,699	4,755,609
1880	3,852,479	3,980,411
1881	3,803,639	4,656,134

Sources: Georgiades 1885, 188–189;
Issawi 1980, 110;
Great Britain, *Accounts and Papers,* 1882–1912.

Table A.1 *(continued)*
Trade of İzmir (Current Pound Sterlings) (1839–1912)

1882	3,841,862	3,215,921
1883	4,710,756	3,238,064
1884	4,820,383	2,928,591
1885	4,315,340	2,692,947
1886	4,331,536	2,706,736
1887	4,099,310	—
1888	3,867,083	2,710,445
1889	4,535,975	3,236,139
1890	3,708,149	3,030,559
1891	3,927,182	2,985,851
1892	3,647,512	3,010,472
1893	3,282,761	—
1894	4,323,839	3,158,263
1895	4,334,097	2,880,727
1896	3,334,000	2,220,000
1897	3,100,000	2,250,000
1898	3,294,529	2,678,000
1899	3,782,781	2,563,000
1900	4,157,405	2,538,000
1901	4,413,370	2,849,000
1902	4,275,233	2,805,000
1903	4,833,931	2,802,000
1904	4,754,533	3,061,000
1905	4,504,162	3,215,000
1906	4,973,412	3,547,000
1907	4,990,107	3,183,000
1908	4,529,830	2,938,000
1909	5,039,000	3,508,000
1910	4,500,000	4,061,000
1911	4,400,000	4,138,000
1912	4,000,000	3,738,000

Sources: Georgiades 1885, 188–189;
Issawi 1980, 110;
Great Britain, *Accounts and Papers,* 1882–1912.

TABLE A.2
Ottoman exports to the U.K., 1840–1876 (£)*

Year	Valonia	%§	Madder Root	%§	Raisins	%§
1840	48,533	3.9	562,017	45.0	37,144	2.9
1841	45,215	3.7	516,120	42.0	36,202	2.9
1842	59,742	5.1	465,377	39.8	14,771	1.2
1843	31,166	2.5	546,286	43.9	34,309	2.7
1844	59,138	4.5	478,766	37.0	34,405	2.6
1845	101,666	6.9	654,203	44.6	60,206	4.1
1846	29,698	2.7	509,501	47.5	22,947	2.1
1847	50,473	2.9	511,147	29.3	28,776	1.6
1848	41,925	2.7	724,940	48.2	19,024	1.2
1849	84,317	4.0	841,893	40.0	21,220	1.0
1850	66,613	2.9	922,856	41.0	17,102	0.7
1851						
1852	76,025	3.3	1,096,398	48.6	65,047	2.8
1853	86,362	2.8	1,012,967	33.2	121,439	3.9
1854						
1855	124,508	6.4	246,107	10.7	107,297	4.6
1856	257,409	10.8	1,303,273	54.6	107,482	4.5
1857	326,570	13.9	402,585	17.1	163,246	6.9
1858	264,876	10.1	400,602	15.3	109,290	4.2
1859	382,347	14.0	430,272	15.7	232,333	8.5
1860	261,501	8.2	421,256	13.2	126,508	3.9
1861	259,935	17.0	394,530	25.8	193,369	12.6
1862	402,668	22.3	326,030	18.1	108,794	6.0
1863	447,641	18.2	311,962	12.6	161,246	6.5
1864	300,683	11.1	258,086	9.0	120,795	4.4
1865	234,846	10.3	189,352	8.3	134,203	5.9
1866	473,730	24.6	289,629	15.0	86,791	4.5
1867	291,181	20.4	182,988	12.8	126,549	8.8
1868	393,433	19.5	398,368	19.7	214,820	10.6
1869	297,230	13.9	224,072	10.5	266,065	12.5
1870	358,407	19.2	154,193	8.2	146,485	7.8
1871	425,323	19.1	152,589	6.8	195,504	8.8
1872	511,972	20.1	98,774	3.8	297,905	11.7
1873	441,429	16.9	42,123	1.6	185,843	7.1
1874	487,937	21.5	104,633	4.6	286,391	12.6
1875	554,416	21.0	41,346	1.5	415,911	15.8
1876	601,266	21.0	17,652	0.6	361,910	12.6

Notes:
(*) The figures for the period 1840–1853 represent official values, for the period 1854–1871 real values, and for 1872–1876 declared values.
(§) Percentage of total exports to the U.K.
(+) Cotton exports refer to cotton yarn until 1857, and to raw cotton after that date.

Source: Cust 4/1840–1876.

Table A.2 *(continued)*
Ottoman exports to the U.K. 1840-876 (£)*

Opium	%§	Cotton	%§	Total Exports	Share of Five Commodities in Total Trade		
7,234	0.5			1,240,812	52.3	1840	Continental Greece
20,806	1.5			1,212,749	50.1	1841	included
7,586	0.6	955	0.08	1,168,036	46.8	1842	(1840-1842)
28,938	2.3	2,428	0.19	1,243,759	51.6	1843	
33,284	2.5	2,615	0.20	1,292,989	46.8	1844	
33,638	2.3	1,431	0.09	1,465,972	57.9	1845	
12,277	1.1	1,620	0.15	1,071,340	53.5	1846	
15,503	0.8	391	0.02	1,739,112	34.6	1847	
26,536	1.7	331	0.02	1,503,961	53.8	1848	Turkish
13,073	0.6	986	0.04	2,102,097	45.6	1849	dominions
16,114	0.7	1,957	0.08	2,250,326	45.3	1850	excluding
				2,511,100		1851	Moldavia,
25,498	1.1	153	0.01	2,252,283	55.8	1852	Wallachia,
19,946	0.6			3,050,518	40.5	1853	Egypt,
				2,219,298		1854	Syria,
72,941	3.1	250	0.01	2,294,571	23.8	1855	Palestine
58,995	2.4	973	0.04	2,383,029	72.3	1856	(1842-1860)
97,934	4.1	465	0.02	2,347,232	42.0	1857	
89,449	3.4	130	0.01	2,604,606	33.0	1858	
133,149	4.8	923	0.03	2,728,354	43.0	1859	
187,643	5.9			3,280,265	31.2	1860	
196,935	12.8	2,704	0.17	1,528,549	68.3	1861	
159,994	8.8	202,520	11.20	1,800,127	56.4	1862	
197,360	8.0	907,679	36.90	2,459,162	82.2	1863	
191,408	7.0	1,366,688	50.50	2,301,860	82.0	1864	Anatolia or
241,362	10.6	1,076,304	47.30	2,274,130	82.4	1865	Asia Minor
146,779	7.6	506,782	26.30	1,925,316	78.0	1866	(1861-1870)
188,703	3.2	220,871	15.4	1,426,702	70.6	1867	
337,209	16.7	122,375	6.0	2,014,201	72.5	1868	
293,615	13.8	354,418	16.6	2,124,707	67.3	1869	
346,274	18.5	235,469	12.6	1,865,137	66.3	1870	
361,970	16.3	73,168	3.2	2,218,992	54.2	1871	
246,501	9.6	213,378	8.3	2,545,531	53.5	1872	Asiatic Turkey
302,201	1.6	199,019	7.6	2,599,148	42.8	1873	including Cyprus,
316,796	13.9	37,969	1.6	2,263,010	54.2	1874	Syria & Turkish
316,243	12.0	27,027	1.0	2,631,373	51.3	1875	Ports on the Persian
221,703	7.7	12,350	0.4	2,854,785	42.3	1876	Gulf (1871-1876)

Notes:
(*) The figures for the period 1840-1853 represent official values, for the period 1854-1871 real values, and for 1872-1876 declared values.
(§) Percentage of total exports to the U.K.
(+) Cotton exports refer to cotton yarn until 1857, and to raw cotton after that date.
Source: Cust 4/1840-1876.

TABLE A.3
Current prices and exports of Valonia in İzmir (1845–1876)

Year	Price s.d./cwt	Quantity Exported cwt
1845	11.10	438,685
1846	10.4	157,628
1847	9.10	224,171
1848	7.0	216,828
1849	8.10	422,857
1850	10.9	309,200
1851	10.3	295,742
1852	10.11	345,771
1853	10.0	369,514
1854	11.9	379,857
1855	12.2	250,085
1856	—	536,828
1857	—	661,742
1858	—	547,885
1859	15.0	749,783
1860	—	510,514
1861	—	480,429
1862	—	718,771
1863	17.4	909,285
1864	18.0	317,400
1865	17.0	425,780
1866	18.0	579,600
1867	20.8	640,000
1868	17.0	757,600
1869	16.0	706,800
1870	12.0	544,000
1871	16.0	425,400
1872	18.0	372,000
1873	17.0	568,000
1874	21.0	632,000
1875	16.0	696,000
1876	18.0	932,220

Sources
Prices
1845–1855: FO 78/652; 701; 750; 795; 832; 868; 905; 954; 1020; 1108; 1209.
    1859: FO 78/1447; 1533.
1863, 1867: Scherzer, 1873: Appendix Figure 5
    1864: FO 78/1888.
1865–1876: Great Britain, *Sessional Papers,* 1867–1877.
Quantity Exported
1845–1869: Cust 4/35–55.
1861–1864: Calculated from *Accounts and Papers.*
1865–1876: Great Britain, *Sessional Papers,* op. cit.

TABLE A.4
Current prices and exports of Madder in İzmir (1845–1876)

Year	Price s.d./cwt	Quantity Exported cwt
1845	45.8	66,755
1846	36.5	52,943
1847	33.10	58,814
1848	27.10	77,182
1849	29.8	99,700
1850	38.8	109,312
1851	34.3	118,387
1852	37.10	119,879
1853	41.4	119,919
1854	38.10	27,383
1855	40.3	93,755
1856	—	101,091
1857	—	134,195
1858	—	153,600
1859	42.2	170,810
1860	—	166,060
1861	—	174,969
1862	—	144,542
1863	48.4	127,402
1864	39.0	105,901
1865	40.0	96,727
1866	35.0	143,265
1867	40.8	—
1868	45.0	147,665
1869	70.0	59,525
1870	64.0	63,046
1871	52.0	54,307
1872	50.0	67,680
1873	50.0	37,305
1874	15.0	72,288
1875	18.0	21,175
1876	16.0	14,602

Sources
Prices
1845–1855: FO 78/652; 701; 750; 795; 832; 868; 905; 954; 1020; 1108.
1859: FO 78/1447; 1533.
1863, 1867: Scherzer 1873: Appendix, Figure 5.
1865–1876: Same as Table A.3.
Quantity Exported
1845–1860: Same as Table A.3.
1861–1876: Same as Table A.3.

TABLE A.5
Current prices and exports of Raisins in İzmir (1845–1876)

Year	Price s.d./cwt	Quantity Exported cwt
1845	16.8	146,313
1846	19.6	55,968
1847	19.7	70,185
1848	17.1	46,400
1849	19.2	51,776
1850	18.6	41,690
1851	13.5	84,866
1852	15.0	158,615
1853	35.4	296,241
1854	25.7	275,666
1855	31.0	155,501
1856	—	90,702
1857	—	110,507
1858	—	94,902
1859	41.6	232,839
1860	—	128,152
1861	24.0	221,445
1862	20.1	135,232
1863	16.0	186,825
1864	20.0	146,758
1865	22.0	161,041
1866	23.0	94,980
1867	17.9	96,226
1868	24.2	258,847
1869	20.8	193,000
1870	22.8	542,000
1871	19.8	548,400
1872	21.0	787,000
1873	21.4	764,000
1874	26.4	620,000
1875	19.4	796,000
1876	17.8	904,000

Sources
Prices
1845–1855: FO 78/652; 701; 750; 795; 832; 868; 905; 954; 1020; 1108; 1209.
1859–1860: FO 78/1447; 1533.
1861–1863: Scherzer 1873, 122.
        1864: FO 78/1888.
1865–1876: Same as Table A.3.
        1867: Scherzer 1873, 122.

Quantity Exported
1845–1860: Same as Table A.3.
1861–1876: Same as Table A.3.

TABLE A.6
Current prices and exports of Opium from İzmir (1840–1876)

Year	Price s.d./lb	Quantity Exported lbs.
1840	3.4	101,494
1841	6.3	301,812
1842	—	110,356
1843	13.10	420,922
1844	14.0	484,144
1845	15.2	489,288
1846	10.4	178,586
1847	10.8	221,320
1848	14.5	385,988
1849	9.9	189,688
1850	10.9	231,788
1851	11.0	200,722
1852	10.5	370,890
1853	10.9	290,126
1854	13.3	—
1855	11.8	204,746
1856	—	149,822
1857	—	250,044
1858	—	180,794
1859	18.3	273,390
1860	—	390,732
1861	—	487,556
1862	—	371,548
1863	19.2	332,250
1864	13.6	372,300
1865	14.9	660,000
1866	17.0	583,350
1867	15.5	318,450
1868	19.0	564,494
1869	42.0	321,809
1870	41.0	278,556
1871	17.0	922,941
1872	28.0	598,214
1873	24.0	472,000
1874	28.0	366,714
1875	16.0	690,625
1876	21.0	294,714

Sources
Prices
1840: Kütükoğlu 1976, 26.
1841: Issawi 1980, 331.
1843–1844: FO 626/7: file: 339.
1845–1855: FO 78/652; 701; 750; 795; 832; 868; 905; 954; 1022; 1108; 1209.
1859: FO 78/1447; 1533.
1863, 1867: Scherzer 1873: Appendix, Figure 4.
1864: FO 78/1888.
1865–1876: Same as Table A.3.
Quantity Exported
1840–1860: Same as Table A.3.
1861–1876: Same as Table A.3.

TABLE A.7
Current prices and export of Cotton from İzmir (1845–1876)

Year	Price s.d./cwt	Quantity Exported cwt
1845	32.4	
1846	35.3	
1847	40.0	
1848	32.10	
1849	37.2	
1850	44.1	
1851	36.0	
1852	36.8	
1853	48.9	
1854	44.0	
1855	49.6	
1856	—	
1857	58.5	11,809
1858	45.10	
1859	—	
1860	—	222,300
1861	—	78,000
1862	149.4	
1863	158.8	234,000
1864	162.5	108,369
1865	121.4	328,640
1866	93.4	136,910
1867	81.8	
1868	74.8	185,400
1869	93.4	132,942
1870	65.4	154,196
1871	84.0	212,928
1872	74.8	216,464
1873	65.4	205,071
1874	56.0	225,618
1875	46.8	241,061
1876	51.4	294,929

Sources
Prices
1845–1862: FO 78/652; 701; 750; 795; 832; 868; 905; 954; 1020; 1108; 1209; 1307;
      1447; 1687.
1863–1864: Scherzer 1873: Appendix, Figure 3.
      1864: FO 78/1831; 1888.
      1867: Scherzer 1873: Appendix, Figure 3.
1868–1876: Same as Table A.3.
Quantity Exported
      1857: Farley 1863: 94.
1860–1861: Owen 1981: 112.
      1863: Ibid.
1864–1870: Same as Table A.3.

Notes

CHAPTER 1

1. See, for example, Eldem 1970; Quataert 1973; Pamuk 1984.

2. The concept of capitalist world economy is developed by Wallerstein and Hopkins. See Wallerstein (1974, 1979, 1980, 1983); Hopkins (1979); Hopkins and Wallerstein (1977, 1981). Also see Braudel 1984, Chap. 1; Arrighi and Drangel 1986.

3. Wallerstein 1979a, 389–390.

4. Weber 1978, 232.

5. Polanyi 1971, 250–256; 1957, 43–55. See also Amin 1976, 51–58.

6. See Kondratieff 1979.

7. See Research Working Group . . . 1979.

8. For a general description of these records, see Kasaba 1985.

CHAPTER 2

1. For the classical system and its key institutions, see İnalcık 1954, 1973, 1975, 1975a; Barkan 1942, 1949–1954, 1980; Güçer 1964, Faroqhi 1977, 1979, 1979a; Itzkowitz 1980.

2. See Wallerstein 1974.

3. Various aspects of this relationship are studies by Lybyer 1915; İnalcık 1973, 121–139; Braudel 1972, 543–556; 1973, 665ff; Braude 1979; Çizakça 1980; Goffman 1985; Turan 1968; Faroqhi 1986; Dames 1921; Hess 1970.

4. See Barkan 1957; Cook 1972.

5. See Sahillioğlu 1978, 12ff.

6. Barkan 1975; Kunt 1983, 80–82.

7. Aymard 1966, 125–135; Braudel 1972, 591–599; McGowan 1981, 34–38.

8. Kunt 1983, 83–84.

9. McGowan 1969.

10. See Wallerstein's assessment of Russia's position in relation to the European world economy in the sixteenth century, 1974, 308–324.

11. Compare İslamoğlu and Faroqhi 1979; Faroqhi 1984, 292.

12. See Wallerstein 1980, 1–34; Braudel and Spooner 1967.

13. The two main types of leases were *malikâne* and *esham*. The former refers to the leasing of a source of revenue in its entirety; the latter, in shares. See Cezar 1986, 33–42, 81, and elsewhere.

14. See Cezar 1986, 104–109.

15. İnalcık 1978, 341–342.

16. See McGowan 1981, 62.

17. Gandev 1960, 210–211.

18. See Stoianovich 1960, 255.

19. See Baer 1970, 1970a.

20. Todorov 1983, 216ff; İnalcık 1980, 50; Pamuk 1984, Chap. 6.

21. See İnalcık 1973, 158–160; Todorov 1983, 217; Genç 1984; Paskaleva 1968, 280.

22. See Kunt 1983, 84–85ff.; McGowan 1981, 57; Rafeq 1977.

23. See Hourani 1968.

24. See İnalcık 1977, 31–37.

25. Kunt 1983, 86–87.

26. See Fleischer 1986, 95–99, 118–123, 180–181, and elsewhere. See also Mumcu 1985, 303–304.

27. For a comprehensive history of the ayan, see Özkaya 1977. See also İnalcık 1977; Nagata 1976; Sadat 1972; Sakaoğlu 1984; Uluçay 1942–1944.

28. İnalcık 1980a, 286.

29. See Stoianovich 1953, 400.

30. İnalcık 1980a, 287–289; McGowan 1981, 150.

31. For examples from various cities, see Stoianovich 1953, 400; Bodman 1963, 8.

32. See İnalcık 1973, 144–146; Mantran 1962, 179–213, 425, 476–492; Kortepeter 1966; Faroqhi 1979a; 1984, 76–82, 288–289; Güçer 1980, 26–28.

33. Wallerstein 1980, 1–34.

34. Genç 1984, 53–55. See also, Cezar 1986, 74.

35. McGowan 1981, 150.

36. Stoianovich 1960, 260; Leon 1972, 30.

37. See Leon 1972, 30.

38. Svoronos 1956, 273–276; McGowan 1981, 14.

39. See Svoronos 1956, 31, 272–274.

40. Shaw 1971, 446.

41. McGowan says that maize was not an important export item from the Balkans (1981, 32). McNeill suggests that while wheat was becoming an export crop, maize was being sown as a replacement in the peasants' diet. He also points out that by virtue of its being a new food, maize was not included among the taxable products of the soil (1964, 205–206). Stoianovich, on the other hand, posits a direct relationship between the expansion of the cultivation of maize and external demand. His sources are primarily contemporary French reports (1953, 404–405).

42. See Svoronos 1956, 239–242; Paskaleva 1968, 275–276.

43. Stoianovich 1960, 260; McGowan 1981, 43.

44. Lampe and Jackson 1982, 35. Still, however, the Ottoman prices were lower than the European prices; hence Ottoman export trade was profitable. See Paskaleva 1968, 280.

45. Stoianovich 1960, 283.

46. Lampe and Jackson 1982, 41; McGowan 1981, 23; Svoronos 1956, 217; Paskaleva 1968, 279.

47. Paskaleva 1968, 274.

48. McGowan 1981, 24; Stoianovich 1960, 260.

49. See map in Svoronos 1956, 403; Paskaleva 1968, 272.

50. The "second" being the one associated with the Civil War in the 1860s (McGowan 1981, 43).

51. See Leon 1972, 41.

52. Leon 1972, 32; Stoianovich 1960, 275.

53. Karpat 1973, 53.

54. Stoianovich 1960, 246.

55. See McNeill 1964, 191–202; 210 221; Karidis 1981.

56. It has been claimed that at the turn of the century there were eighty Turkish commercial establishments in Vienna, with a capital of at least ten thousand florins each; see Paskaleva 1968, 274.

57. Chapman 1977, 35–38.

58. Lampe and Jackson 1982, 45.

59. Lampe and Jackson 1982, 45–46; Todorov 1983, 314.

60. Lampe and Jackson 1982, 46–47; Stoianovich 1960, 250–254.

61. Stoianovich 1960, 234.

62. Issawi 1977, 157; Lampe and Jackson 1982, 38.

63. See McGowan 1981, 90–94; 133–134.

64 Stoianovich 1960, 248–249.

65. Stoianovich 1960, 248–249; Karpat 1982, 155–156.

66. See Cezar 1986, 74–142.

67. Cezar 1986, 89–91, 137–138.

68. Cezar 1986, 138–40.

69. İnalcık 1980a, 296; Todorov 1983, 136.

70. Issawi 1980, 326–331.

71. Stoianovich 1960, 302.

72. See Todorov 1983, Chaps. 12 and 13.

73. Çiftlik agriculture has rightly been in the center of most of the works dealing with the social transformation in the Balkans. Over the years, a fairly consistent body of literature has accumulated. Much of the following information derives from: Stoianovich 1953; Gandev 1960; Veinstein 1976; McGowan 1981; İnalcık 1983.

74. Busch-Zantner 1938; Stoianovich 1953.

75. Nagata 1976a; McGowan 1981; İnalcık 1983.

76. McGowan 1981, 165.

77. Gandev 1960, 208.

78. İnalcık 1983, 117.

79. McGowan 1981, 164; Lampe and Jackson 1982, 35.

80. The classical system included provisions that accorded freehold status to such lands and granted rights of ownership to their developers. See İnalcık 1983, 108-111; and Barkan 1980, 151-154.

81. McGowan 1981, 73-79. According to Gandev, wealthy farmers formed their own commercial associations and went into export business on their own (1960, 211). See also Paskaleva 1968, 277; Berend and Ranki 1982, Chap. 1.

82. İnalcık 1978, 342-346; McGowan 1981, 147-155; Özkaya 1974, passim.

83. See Özkaya 1974, 450-451.

84. McGowan 1981, 146.

85. Stoianovich 1953, 403.

86. McGowan 1981, 70.

87. Stoianovich 1953, 405.

88. Gandev 1960, 202; McGowan 1981, 64.

89. İnalcık 1983, 116-119, 120/121; Stoianovich 1953.

90. Gandev 1960, 213-215.

91. See Stoianovich 1953, 403-404.

92. McGowan 1981, 76-77.

93. Gandev 1960, 211; see also Veinstein 1976.

94. For a comprehensive account, see Issawi 1982.

95. See Stoianovich 1960, 235–239; Lybyer 1915; İnalcık 1960, 1969.

96. Issawi 1982, 262–263.

97. On this point, see İslamoğlu and Keyder 1977.

98. Issawi 1982, 263.

99. Clogg 1982, 185–190; Karpat 1973, 70ff.

100. Leon 1972, 42.

101. Leon 1972, 29–30, 42–43; Todorov 1983, 98–99.

102. Karpat 1973, 53.

103. Karpat 1973, 57ff.

104. Stavrianos 1958, 245.

105. Karidis 1981.

106. Leon 1972, 44.

107. Stoianovich 1960, 234.

108. Clogg 1981a; Stavrianos 1958, 279–282.

109. Stoianovich 1960, 306.

110. Various aspects of the Balkan nationalism have been studied by Stavrianos 1958; Jelavich and Jelavich 1977; Sugar and Lederer 1969; Clogg 1981; Karpat 1973; Haddad and Ochsenwald 1977.

111. See Karpat 1973, 93ff; in 1821, the Holy Synod in Istanbul issued a letter anathematizing the Philiki Etairia; see Clogg 1976, 203–206. However, this did not save them from losing many of their privileges at the Porte. Lewis 1965, 288–289.

112. Karpat 1982, 153–155; Chirot 1976, 112–117.

113. İnalcık has a different interpretation of the Pledge of Alliance. He argues that this document was an attempt at legitimizing and institutionalizing the feudal status of the big landlords (1964a, 607). My interpretation follows Mardin 1969.

114. Abou-el Haj 1974; Hurewitz 1961.

115. İnalcık 1971, 1185; Hurewitz 1975, 71–74.

116. Hurewitz 1975, 92–101; Karpat 1973, 52ff.

117. Stoianovich 1960, 288.

118. See Lewis 1960. According to one survey, by 1808 Russia alone had enrolled 120,000 Greeks as "protected persons." Inalcık 1971, 1186. See also Bağış 1983, passim; esp. 40–50.

119. Findley 1980, 183–190; Bağış 1983, 57–59.

120. See Findley 1980, 34–55; 139; 349.

121. See Bailey 1970, 46–47; Anderson 1966, 79–80.

122. Hurewitz 1975, 126–133.

123. Hurewitz 1975, 162; Stavrianos 1958, 202–206.

124. Hurewitz 1975, 107.

125. See Bailey 1970, 46–47, 56; Anderson 1966, 79–80.

126. See Hurewitz 1975, 279; Anderson 1966, 106–107; Puryear 1969, 176ff.

CHAPTER 3

1. Quoted in Blaisdell 1966, 26.

2. See Davis 1979, 15.

3. Davis 1979, 18, 59.

4. See Schlote 1951, 46, 47, 78–79; Hobsbawm 1968, 144; Imlah 1958, 100.

5. See Jenks 1973, Chaps. II–IV.

6. Jenks 1973, 61, 159.

7. See Fairlie 1969, 101.

8. Between 1828 and 1841, annual consumption per capita of domestic wheat declined from 7.92 to 7.84 bushels, whereas that of imported what increased from 0.40 to 0.88 bushels. Fairlie 1969, 102.

9. Hobsbawm 1968, 77.

10. For various discussions, see Semmel 1970.

11. Imlah 1958, 154; Supple 1978, 321.

12. Imlah 1958, 193–194; Youngson 1966, 173–174; Supple 1978, 339–340.

13. Imlah 1958, 190–191; Schlote 1951, 81; see Clapham 1968, 135; Cole and Deane 1966, 51–52; Woodruff 1973, 659.

14. Gallagher and Robinson 1953, 11.

15. Between 1831 and 1840, world gold production stood at 20,300 kg, whereas between 1866 and 1870, 191,000 kg of gold was produced. Hobsbawm 1979, 346. Only in the United States did gold production rise from less than one million dollars a year in value in 1841–45 to an average of 51.2 million dollars a year in 1856–60. Imlah 1958, 157–158, n. 3.

16. Jenks 1973, 161.

17. For example, between 1856 and 1860 almost all of the gold produced in the United States was exported. Imlah 1958, 157–158, n. 3.

18. Bullion reserves of the Bank of England jumped from £8.3 in October 1847 to an average of £21.8 million in the third quarter of 1852; that of the Bank of France from 122.6 francs in 1847 to 584.8 million francs in 1852. Landes 1966, 433.

19. About 50% of the new gold produced from 1850–55 (estimated at £858.9 million) went into monetary stocks. Imlah 1958, 157, note 2. Issues of paper money increased on the strength of the growing stock of bullion. Note circulation of the Bank of France more than tripled, rising from 450 million francs in 1850 to 1,550 million in 1870, while that of the Preussichie Bank shot upward from 18,370 million thaler in 1850 to 163,260 million in 1870. Landes 1966, 432.

20. Between 1850 and 1873, wholesale price indexes increased from 91 to 130 in England, 110 to 144 in France, and 75 to 120 in Germany (1913=100). Mitchell 1981, 737. This monetarist explanation has been widely debated, and the reliability of price indexes have been questioned by various economic historians (for a summary see Church 1979, 13–22). But, whatever the short-term rhythms and the temporality of the price trends might have been, that the mid-Victorian period as a whole constituted an "inflationary interlude in a deflationary century" is not generally disputed. See Church 1979, 16.

21. See Church 1979, 65–70.

22. Hobsbawm 1979, 55.

23. Landes 1966, 429.

24. See Robbins 1962; Girard 1966.

25. See Girard 1966, 245; Born 1983, Chap. III.

26. Telegraph lines quickly multiplied in Europe: in 1849 there were 2,000 miles; in 1854 15,000; in 1859 42,000; in 1864 80,000; in 1869 111,000; Hobsbawm 1979, 59–60.

27. Polanyi 1957, Chap. 1; also see Fisher 1966; Hobsbawm 1979, 126–127.

28. Gallagher and Robinson 1953, 8.

29. Hobsbawm 1962, 113.

30. In Hobsbawm's words, "it was now known that revolution in a single country could be a European phenomenon, that its doctrines could spread across the frontiers and . . . its crusading armies could blow away the political systems of a continent. It was now known that social revolution was possible; that nations existed as something independent of states, peoples as something independent of their rulers and even that poor existed as something independent of the ruling class." Hobsbawm 1962, 117.

31. Hobsbawm 1962, 137–146.

32. See Hobsbawm 1979, 75; Supple 1978, 321. In 1850, universal male suffrage was practiced for the first time in France. Hobsbawm 1979, 106–125.

33. About the Crimean War, see n. 62 below. Also see Todorova 1977, 40; Anderson 1961, 47; Puryear 1969, 223–226.

34. Polanyi 1957, 6, 259–62.

35. See Hobsbawm 1962, 139; 1979, 106–125.

36. Bairoch 1973, 8.

37. See Hobsbawm 1968, 139; 1979, 48–50; Ashworth 1962, 205–206; Woodruff 1973, 658; Hanson 1980, 14.

38. See Fairlie 1969; Ashworth 1962, 206; Woodruff 1973, 657–671; Berend and Ranki 1982, 21ff. As an indication of the new pattern of specialization, we can cite the substantial increase in the world trade in grains that stood at 2 million tons in 1840 but had reached 11.2 million tons in 1870. Hobsbawm 1979, 50. Also see Friedmann 1978, 554. On regional variations, see Dovring 1966; Landes 1966, 431; Bairoch 1974.

39. Landes 1966, 455–456.

40. Between 1835 and 1860 in western Europe, the output of producers goods grew more than three times as fast as that of the consumer goods. Cole and Deane 1966, 19.

41. See Frank 1978, 178; Woodruff 1973, 672; Paish 1949, 51.

42. Cole and Deane 1966, 15ff, 27–29; Youngson 1966, 156–160; Berend and Ranki 1982, Chap. II; Dovring 1966.

43. Landes 1966, 456–460.

44. See Emmanuel 1972.

45. See Youngson 1966, 146; Friedmann 1978.

46. See Landes 1966, 430-431; Wolf 1982, 318-322.

47. Frank 1978, 190ff.

48. Landes 1966, 430-431; Hobsbawm 1968, 136; also Berend and Ranki 1982, 39.

49. Glass and Grebenik 1966, 62ff; Dovring 1966, 606-607, 613-616.

50. Chirot 1976, 161-162.

51. This includes net inflows from direct investments and foreign loans. Based on Pamuk 1984, 163, 167.

52. Pamuk 1984, 30.

53. See Hurewitz 1975, 320; Anderson 1966, 143.

54. See Pamuk 1984, 25-26.

55. Pamuk 1984, 25-26; Kurmuş 1974, 39.

56. In 1794-96, the share of the Near East in British exports was only 0.4%; whereas in 1854-56, Britain was selling 6% of its exports in the Ottoman Empire. See Davis 1979, 59.

57. Leon 1972, 32.

58. Puryear 1969, 124-125; Issawi 1980, 75.

59. İnalcık 1980, 43-45; Wood 1964, 170; Bailey 1970, 40-41, 43, 65.

60. See İnalcık 1980, 45.

61. Pamuk 1984, 140.

62. This was accomplished in two stages: first, through the settlement of the Egyptian problem in an international conference in London (see Puryear 1969, 176-179; Anderson 1966, 106-107; Hurewitz 1975, 279); second, with the Crimean War and the Paris Peace Treaty (see Kütükoğlu 1976, 39 41; Anderson 1961, 45; Anderson 1966, 142-143; Puryear 1969, 220-222; Hurewitz 1975, 320).

63. See Pamuk 1984, 27, 140; Feis 1939, 317ff.

64. See Issawi 1980, 77; Kütükoğlu 1976, 26-27; Stelle 1940; Kurmuş 1974, 85-87.

65. Shaw 1975; Cezar 1986, 282-291.

66. Barkan 1980, 319-322.

67. Cezar 1986, 295; Davison 1980.

68. Issawi 1980, 327; Du Velay 1978, 72.

69. Du Velay 1978, 72-74.

70. Du Velay 1978, 71. *Türk Ziraat Tarihine Bir Bakış* 1938, 233; Güran n.d., 115-129; Michelsen 1853, 186-187.

71. See Shaw 1975, 421; İnalcık 1964b, 628-631; Suvla 1966, 97.

72. See Çadırcı 1980; Bağış 1982, 87-96; Findley 1980, 128.

73. See İnalcık 1977, 35-40.

74. Shaw 1969, 60-63; Ortaylı 1985, 29-45.

75. İnalcık 1964b, 625-627.

76. Davison 1963, 146ff.

77. See Senior 1859, 45; Davison 1963, 146ff; Shaw 1975, 426-427; Findley 1980, 167-190.

78. See Barkan 1980, 337-340.

79. Davison 1963, 126-131; Karpat 1982, 162-163.

80. See Bailey 1970, Chap. IV.

81. In the 1840s the Ottoman government sponsored the establishment of a line of factories in İstanbul, primarily to supply the growing needs of the army (see Ökçün 1972). This has prompted some analysts to hail an "Ottoman Industrial Revolution" (Clark 1974). None of these ventures was strong enough to survive without heavy subsidies by the government, which the latter was unable to provide on a long-term basis. Consequently, all these enterprises went bankrupt within a few years of their establishment, which undermines the credibility of the exaggerated claims regarding their long-term significance. See also Ahmad 1984.

82. For example, Marx was quite surprised at the enthusiastic support for Turkey that was voiced in especially the liberal press in England. In 1853, he wrote, "[*The Daily Press*] goes on dithyrambic strain, so far as *The Daily Press* can be dithyrambic, with an apotheosis of Turkey, the Turks, and everything Turkish which must appear quite incomprehensible to most of its readers." (1952, 136.) The perennial Turcophile was, of course, David Urquhart, an employee of the British Foreign Office (see Urquhart 1833). His support for the Ottoman empire prompted Marx to remark that "If Mr. Urquhart was not a

British subject he would decidedly prefer being a Turk; if he was not a Presbyterian Calvinist, he would not belong to any other religion than Islamism; and [according to him] . . . Britain and Turkey are the only two countries in the world to enjoy self government, and social and religious liberty." (1952, 137).

83. Du Velay 1978, 80; Rodkey 1958, 351; Cevdet 1953, 21–22.

84. Suvla 1966, 99.

85. Bailey 1970, 77; Du Velay 1978, 70–71; Anderson 1964.

86. Işıksal 1968.

87. See Blaisdell 1966, 26.

88. Tengirşenk 1940, 289; Puryear 1969, 125ff; Issawi 1980, 76.

89. For the text, see Issawi 1966, 39–40; Kütükoğlu 1976, 4–6; Also see Puryear 1969, 124–125; Issawi 1980, 75.

90. Suvla 1966, 96; Aktan 1966, 109.

91. See Poroy 1981.

92. This interpretation of the effects of the 1838 treaties is different from the more conventional approaches. For example, compare Köymen 1971. For a line of argument that is closer to the one contained here, see Kurmuş 1981; Keyder 1981.

93. Senior 1859, 132. Ahmet Vefik Pasha, Ottoman minister of education, expressed the concern of his government to Senior as follows: "When we gave to you the full liberty of trade, we meant commerce not retail trade. We meant that you might bring in cloth or leather, not that you might be our tailors or shoemakers. We meant you to bring us wine and gin in barrels not to open spirit shops in breach of our religion and our laws, and to corrupt and poison our people" (1859, 135–136).

94. See Sarç 1966, 54; Issawi 1966, 46.

95. Findley 1980, 14–15; 36.

96. Mardin 1962 remains as the best account of the New Ottoman movement.

97. Cited in Findley 1980, 379 n. 40; see also 163–185; Senior 1859, 84–85, 107.

98. Consequently, the operations of the better known councils of the Tarzimat era such as the Council of State (*Şuray-ı Devlet*), Council of Reforms (*Meclisi Âli-i Tanzimat*), and the Council of Judicial Ordinances (*Divan-ı Ahkâm-ı*

Adliyye) were overwhelmingly centralized in Istanbul. Those that extended their presence beyond the capital city, such as the Council of Reconstruction (*Meclisi Imariyye*) and the Commission of Provincial Inspection (*Vilayet Tetkik Komisyonu*) were still based on the same principle in that they were composed of bureaucrats from Istanbul assessing the situation in the provinces and reporting back to the Porte. See Gökbilgin 1967, 103–104; Findley 1980, 172–177; Davison 1963, 104–107, 142–151; Lewis 1976, 112–113.

99. See Velidedeoğlu 1940; Davison 1963, 68 n. 50, 73, 263; Barkan 1980, 337.

100. Karpat 1982, 163.

101. Cited in Davison 1963, 35. For other examples, see Mumcu 1985, 101, 134, 287–289, 293–294, and elsewhere.

102. Devereux 1963, 147–153; 261–273; Findley 1980, 226.

103. FO 195/241: 209, 4 April 1845.

104. See Senior 1859, 177–178.

105. See Ortaylı 1985, 67–91; Shaw 1969.

106. Here, too, the Ottoman government was supported by the British, who opposed constitutionalism in the Ottoman Empire on grounds that it would enfeeble the central government. See Temperley 1933.

107. By some accounts, the growth of İzmir as a commercial center dates from as early as the sixteenth century. See Goffman 1985. For the eighteenth century, see Issawi 1966, 36; Kurmuş 1974, 41; Paris 1957, 447. See also Frangakis 1984; Ülker 1974.

108. Quataert 1973, 96; see also Eldem 1970, 270/271 and 306–307; Sahillioğlu 1968, 61.

109. Keyder 1983a, 132; Güran n.d., 27; Pamuk 1984, 88.

110. See Pamuk 1984, 88–102.

111. Güran n.d., 82.

112. Pamuk 1984, 88.

113. Issawi 1980, 202.

114. See Gerber 1987, 22–30.

115. FO 78/402: 169–174, 10 January 1840.

116. FO 78/490: 238–247, 10 February 1842.

117. FO 78/1307: 275, 5 December 1857.

118. Issawi 1980, 203.

119. Issawi 1980, 203.

120. Issawi 1980, 207.

121. Karpat 1983; Akbal 1951.

122. FO 78/868: 94–103, 13 March 1851.

123. FO 78/612: 269–280, 26 April 1845; FO 78/1450: 72, Report on Agriculture in Bursa, 1858; FO 78/1609: 55, 31 January 1861; FO 78/1686: 63, 26 February 1862.

124. On wages, see Boratav et al. 1985.

125. Yannoulopoulos 1981, 31.

126. See Veinstein 1976, 76. See also İnalcık 1983.

127. Veinstein 1976, 76.

128. See Gould 1976.

129. In 1841, Consul Sandison reported, "Soil falls in the hands of peasants without any middle class of farmers possessed of capital to portion out the land on lease or purchase." FO 78/441: 240–245, 28 January 1841.

130. FO 78/532: 59, 18 February 1843; see also Issawi 1980, 202, 207.

131. FO 78/442: 114–115, 6 December 1841.

132. FO 78/532: 59–68, 18 February 1843.

133. FO 78/905: 69, 12 August 1852.

134. Ubicini 1856, 319.

135. Issawi 1980, 207.

136. Issawi 1980, 205.

137. Issawi 1980, 205–206.

138. FO 78/905: 18, 30 April 1852.

139. FO 78/1687: 181, 26 July 1862; FO 78/1760: 146, 23 June 1863; FO 78/1831: 201, 7 October 1864; 224–225, 17 October 1864.

140. Quoted in Davison 1963, 302.

141. Quataert 1973, 36.

142. Prior to this decree, the rate of the tithe had been 1.8 in the European provinces; 1/4 + 1/15 in Malatya; 2.5/20 in Aydın, etc. Barkan 1980, 321.

143. Barkan 1980, 322.

144. Quataert 1973, 32-33; Akarlı 1976, 160-164.

145. See Aktan 1966.

146. Ibid.; Akarlı 1976, 154-155.

147. FO 195/241: 213-218, 15 April 1845.

148. Ibid.

149. FO 78/905: 19, 30 April 1852.

150. FO 78/795: 99, April 1849.

151. FO 78/1609: 67, 31 January 1861. Also, FO 195/299: 217-232, 10 January 1848; FO 78/1209: 91, 5 March 1856; FO 78/1533: 277-278, 28 July 1860; and Issawi 1980: 23.

152. The very first document of the first volume of the Records of the İzmir Court of the mid-nineteenth century is a copy of an imperial ferman reminding the court officials of the Sultan's "previous orders to take utmost care to provide for the security of especially [his] non-Muslim subjects." IMS, I:1, 1853/54. For a copy, see Kasaba 1985.

153. For example, in 1854 when a non-Muslim failed to pay a debt of 2,000 kuruş to a Muslim in nine months, the court approved the expropriation of his olive oil press valued at 5,000 kuruş by the lender. IMS, I:27, 1854/55. For other examples, see Kasaba 1985.

154. For example, when a Muslim died he or she "moved from a temporary form of existence to a permanent one"; whereas non-Muslims simply "exhausted" themselves. IMS, I:4, 1853/54.

155. In some instances estates were divided into as many as 128 shares. For example, a case from 1845 in IMS, I:33, 1845.

156. Cezar 1986, 183-192.

157. Cezar 1986, 252.

158. Cezar 1986, 223-224.

159. *Türk Ziraat Tarihine Bir Bakış* 1938, 128-139.

160. FO 78/1307: 272-286, 5 December 1857; Also see Kurmuş 1987.

161. FO 78/1391: 9–10, 3 April 1858.

162. See Quataert 1973, Chaps. VIII–XII.

163. As early as 1848, the British consul in İzmir observed that it "[would] be in vain to expect any amelioration in the condition of the people who are still as much oppressed by the local authorities in this port of Asia Minor as they were previous to the promulgation of the Hatt-ı Şerif which remains a complete dead letter as far as they are concerned." FO 195/288: 352, 15 September 1848.

164. Karpat 1985, 60–77.

165. FO 78/652: 108, 25 May 1846.

166. FO 78/652: 94–100, 14 March 1846; FO 195/797: 106–108.

167. FO 195/299: 356, 2 May 1849.

168. FO 78/832: 52, 64, 27 February 1850; 67ff., 15 April 1850.

169. FO 78/952: 259–65 Report on Agriculture in Bursa, 1852; FO 78/1450: 125–127, 15 March 1859; FO 78/1609: 55, 31 January 1861.

170. FO 78/905: 35–36, 19 June 1852; FO 195/299: 356, 2 May 1849.

171. Pamuk 1984, 191.

172. Karpat 1978, 258; Cuinet 1892, 347.

173. Uluçay and Gökçen 1939, 55–59; Uluçay 1942–1944.

174. Various information about governors can be found in FO 78/1391, 1447, 1533, 1606, 1760.

175. FO 78/1533: 201, 210, 19 May 1860; 2 June 1860.

176. FO 78/1760, 18 April 1863.

177. Great Britain, *Sessional Papers,* 1871, Vol. LXV, pp. 545–551.

178. FO 195/288: 11, 18 February 1847. The actual number given in this document, excluding families, is 8,768. This includes 3,376 Greeks, 2,258 British, 2,000 Austrians, 356 French, 294 Scandinavians, 286 Neapolitians, 90 Russians, 89 Dutch, and 19 Prussians. I multiplied this number by two to account for families and dependents.

179. Issawi 1980, 34.

180. Farley 1862, 79–80.

181. Cuinet 1892, 439.

182. FO 78/1533: 304, 28 July 1860.

183. Farley 1862, 78–80.

184. FO 78/1533: 304, 28 July 1860.

185. Platt 1971, 140–144; also, Senior 1859, 118–119.

186. Platt 1971, 157, 163; and Iseminger 1968.

187. BT 1/569. See also Toprak 1982, 135.

188. FO 195/177: 536, 28 January 1843.

189. Petition dated 10 July 1840, in FO 195/177: 134–136.

190. FO 78/1606: 356–362, 12 November 1861; FO 78/1687: 27–28, 14 January 1862.

191. FO 78/1209: 410, 29 May 1856; 451, 26 July 1856.

192. Great Britain, *Sessional Papers*, 1873, LXVII: 753.

193. Farley 1862, 80.

194. FO 626 Series in Public Record Office contains the records of bankruptcy proceedings against many foreign residents. For example, G. Maltass owed over 8 million kr. when he went bankrupt in 1853 (FO 626/1); F. Whittall's debts were over 800,000 kr. when he went bankrupt in 1861 (FO 626/3).

195. Kurmuş 1974, 101–102.

196. Long before the passing of the decree in 1867, foreign subjects had purchased land in western Anatolia either by getting special permission from the government or in partnership with Ottoman subjects. For example, in 1840, an English merchant from İstanbul purchased five thousand acres of land around Bursa and "brought in adequate stocks of ploughs and farming equipment from England." FO 78/441: 240–245, 28 January 1841. Similar investments were made during the cotton boom of the early 1860s, but none of these turned out to be long-term ventures. FO 78/1533: 273–276, 28 July 1860.

197. Cuinet 1892, 439.

198. FO 78/1986: 254, 31 December 1867.

199. Great Britain, *Sessional Papers*, 1870, LXIV: 80.

200. Georgiades 1885, 155ff.

201. Kurmuş 1974, 69–73.

202. *The Times*, 6 January 1905, quoted in Quataert 1981, 77.

203. See Chapter 4.

204. FO 78/442: 16, 21 January 1841.

205. FO 195/241: 103-106, 25 August 1843.

206. FO 78/571: 39, 25 May 1844.

207. FO 195/288: 712, 1 August 1849.

208. FO 78/795: 180-181, 31 December 1848.

209. Rougon 1892, 684-685. Issawi 1980, 101.

210. BT 1/569.

211. Great Britain, *Sessional Papers*, 1873, LXVII:751.

212. See, for example, Kazgan 1977; Du Velay 1978, 72-74.

213. Jenks 1973, 296-297; Landes 1958, 27.

214. Chapman 1977, 37.

215. Ubicini 1856a, 314.

216. See Du Velay 1978, 72ff.

217. See Akarlı 1976, 165-167; Issawi 1980, 339.

218. FO 78/1302: 321, 18 February 1857.

219. This is why when the peasantry was pressured, they filed their complaints and grievances directly with the government. See Akarlı 1976, 158-159.

220. Urquhart 1833, 110-111.

221. Ubicini 1856, 330.

222. Great Britain, *Sessional Papers*, 1873, LXVII: 752.

223. FO 78/490: 212-237, 10 February 1842.

224. Farley 1862, 81, 98, 103.

225. FO 78/1686: 65-66, 26 February 1862.

226. FO 195/288: 819-821, 30 October 1849; FO 195/350: 9-10, December (?) 1849.

227. FO 195/299: 217, 10 January 1848.

228. Turgay 1981-1985, 66-67, 82.

229. See Ubicini 1856a, 315.

230. FO 78/868: 94–103, January (?) 1851.

231. FO 78/1302: 342–343, February (?) 1857.

232. FO 78/1302: 347, February (?) 1857.

233. See Ubicini 1856a, 315.

234. Urquhart 1833, 110; Cezar 1986, 242–43.

235. Great Britain, *Sessional Papers,* 1873, LXVII: 754.

236. For examples, see Cezar 1986, 126, 136.

237. Du Velay 1978, 90–91; see also Suvla 1966, 96ff; and Davison 1980.

238. FO 195/350: 168, 28 June 1850.

239. FO 78/1760: 96–102, 25 April 1863.

240. FO 195/350: 66–67, 20 March 1850.

241. Ubicini 1856, 283.

242. Ubicini 1856, 282. See also Abdul-Rahman & Nagata 1977, 187ff.

243. See Issawi 1980, 341; Güran n.d., 130; Farley 1862, 100.

244. Had it been carried out, this loan would have greatly eased the shortage of currency in the empire; see Du Velay 1978, 89ff.

245. FO 78/1686: 65, 26 February 1862.

246. Issawi 1980, 341.

247. Calculated from FO 78/1447: 46–89; 1533: 106–138; 1606: 86–127, Return of the Civil Suits for the years 1858, 1859, 1860, respectively.

248. For examples, see FO 78/1398: 153, 17 October 1858.

249. FO 78/1111: 27–36, January (?) 1855.

250. FO 78/1398: 67, 12 April 1858.

251. FO 78/1450: 68–70, Report on the Trade of Bursa, 1858.

252. FO 78/1450: 181–186, 3 June 1859.

253. FO 195/288: 54--543, 13 May 1849.

254. FO 78/905: 78–83, 12 September 1852.

255. FO 78/1398: 157–168, 28 November 1858.

256. FO 78/1450: 11–12, 12 January 1859.

257. Issawi 1980, 329–331.

258. FO 78/1111: 27–36, January (?) 1855.

259. See Poroy 1981, 195; Georgiades 1885, 16.

260. Georgiades 1885, 24–25.

261. FO 78/1307: 275 (Replies to the queries put by the Cotton Supply Association of Manchester relative to the cultivation of Cotton in the Jurisdiction of [İzmir] Consulate, 5, Dec. 1857).

262. FO 78/1534: 30–39, 13 October 1860.

263. Issawi 1980, 248.

264. FO 78/1760: 121–128, 23 May 1863.

265. Güran n.d., 37.

266. Güran n.d., 79.

267. Georgiades 1885, 13, 16, 27, 46.

268. FO 78/868: 94–103, 13 March 1851.

269. FO 78/1609: 67, 31 January 1861. After 1855, Muslim women started to take employment in filatures in Bursa even though they had to mix unveiled with men at work. FO 78/1111: 44–50, 24 January 1855; 168, 13 August 1855. In 1861, the filatures in Bursa employed 2,600 females as opposed to 200 males. FO 78/1686: 62, 26 February 1862. It must be noted that from a strictly agricultural perspective, female employment could not have led to a significant rise in the available work force since women had always been an integral part of the labor force in Anatolian agriculture.

270. FO 78/1533: 273–276, 28 July 1860.

CHAPTER 4

1. See Table 4; Appendix, Table A.1.

2. Pamuk 1984, 30–31.

3. Rougon 1892, 530; Issawi 1980, 134.

4. Georgiades 1885, 187; Rougon 1892, 265. In all instances, the commodities included in Ottoman exports were overwhelmingly composed of foodstuffs and

primary materials of agricultural origin. See Rougon 1892, 269–273; Gordon 1932, 49; Kançal 1983, 394.

5. See Table 4. Also Issawi 1980, 110; Georgiades 1884, 187.

6. Quataert 1973, 18; Issawi 1980, 77.

7. See Appendix, Table A.2.

8. See Kütükoğlu 1976, 38–42.

9. Issawi 1980, 200, 206, 211, 213.

10. For example, in 1845, because of a crop failure, 440,000 bushels (approximately 55,000 quarters) of grain was imported into Gemlik, on the southern coast of the Marmara Sea, from the "Russian ports on the Black Sea." FO 78/652: 84, 30 March 1846. Also in FO 78/442: 114–115, 6 December 1841.

11. After the 1880s, with the completion of the Anatolian railways, cereal production in and exports from central Anatolia increased noticeably, but was reversed again shortly thereafter (Quataert 1973, 381).

12. See Appendix, Table A.2; Kurmuş 1974, 152; Eldem 1970, 135; Georgiades 1885, 45.

13. Fairlie 1964, 497; Urquhart 1833, 176. Before the 1860s, British madder imports varied in annual value in the range of £750,000 to £1,000,000; Lilley 1978, 243.

14. Lilley 1978, 243–244.

15. See Appendix, Table A.2.

16. See Turgay 1981–1985; Stelle 1940; Poroy 1981; Kütükoğlu 1976, 25 and elsewhere.

17. Appendix, Table A.2; Poroy 1981, 198; Georgiades 1885, 15.

18. See Kurmuş 1987, 161.

19. See Appeldix, Table A.2.

20. See Goffman 1985, 198; Kurmuş 1987, 160.

21. The replies of the British consul in İzmir are in FO 78/1307, 5 December 1857.

22. FO 78/1760: 137–46, 23 June 1863; Kurmuş 1974, 85, and 1987, 164ff.

23. Georgiades 1885, 11.

24. Georgiades 1885, 12; Rougon 1892, 96–97, 271.

25. Quataert 1973, 217.

26. Issawi 1980, 264.

27. Quataert 1981, 72.

28. See Appendix, Table A.2.

29. See Quataert 1973, 217–236; Georgiades 1885, 23–24.

30. In interpreting numerical representations of the various sectors of the Ottoman economy in the nineteenth century, including the price series included in this chapter and in the Appendix, the reader should be aware of a number of limitations and some inherent problems in the available data. For a discussion, see Appendix.

31. For example, between 1855–59 and 1860–64, prices of raw cotton increased by about 209%, whereas the rise in the prices of cotton manufactures exported by Britain between these years was about 84% (Imlah 1958, 209–210). Relatively, raw cotton exports constituted a larger share of the total exports from İzmir than did the cotton manufactures in the imports. In 1864, the relevant figures were as follows:

Total exp. from İzmir : £3,842,285		Total imp. to İzmir : £2,538,228	
Cotton exports	: £1,268,920	Cotton mnf. imports : £ 311,986	
%:	33	%:	12

(FO 78/1888: 194-196.)

On terms of trade, see also Pamuk 1984, 44–47.

32. Jean Baptist Giraud vs. J. B. Peterson, FO 626/7, file 339.

33. For an elaboration of these, see Chapter 3; see also Keyder 1983, 64–70. Since it is not possible to obtain precise data, I estimated the volume of agricultural production from the current prices and quantities of exports of valonea, madder, raisin, opium, and cotton. The first step here was to determine the distribution of agricultural production between exports and local consumption. Contemporary reports (Consular Correspondance in the FO 78 series, Farley 1862, Scherzer 1873, Georgiades 1885, Rougon 1892) and various modern accounts (Quataert 1973, Kurmuş 1974, Pamuk 1984) suggest that until the mid-nineteenth century about 60% of locally grown valonea was exported; after 1850 this percentage went up to about 80%; during the middle decades of the nineteenth century, most of the madder was picked for export; raisins that were

exported corresponded to about one half of total grape production; and for opium and cotton the share of exports in total production was 80 and 75% respectively. By using these percentages and with the general assumption of an overall ratio of commodification of about 50% in western Anatolia, I calculated the constant value of agricultural production for the five-year intervals and tabulated the results in Table 6. (For further details see Kasaba 1986: 375–385).

34. Pamuk 1984, 140.

35. The only estimate is that of Pamuk's and covers the entire 1860–1914 period. According to him, there was a twofold increase in commodity production in agriculture in the Ottoman Empire in that period. See Pamuk 1984, 80; also see Quataert 1973, 21–23.

36. Kurmuş 1974, 68.

37. By a margin that was as high as 3.2 million pounds in 1865. See Appendix, Table A.1. In this respect, İzmir was unique among the major ports of the Ottoman Empire; see Issawi 1980, 82.

38. Farley 1862, 97–99; Issawi 1980, 338–339.

39. In 1872, total tithe revenue of the Ottoman government was 434,290,930 kr. (Shaw 1975, 452). In that year, İzmir is estimated to have raised 37–44 million kr. in tithe revenues (Scherzer 1873, 37–38). During the same year, total revenues of the Ottoman government and İzmir province were 1,920,081,000 kr. and 134,900,000 kr., respectively. (Shaw 1975, 451; Scherzer 1873, 39).

40. Scherzer 1873, 39; Quataert 1973, 18.

41. See FO 78/490: 248–258, 19 February 1842.

42. In the Ottoman Empire as late as 1911 per capita consumption of cotton and sugar were 2.66 kg and 6.8 kg per year, respectively; for England these figures were 19 and 37.7 kg. Pamuk 1984, 111; Ortaylı 1983, 168.

43. Aktan 1966, 111; Quataert 1981.

44. For an estimate of the 1850 budget, see Ubicini 1856, 284; for the subsequent budgets and their analyses, see *Türk Ziraat Tarihi* . . . 1938, Appendices; Du Velay 1978, 111; Aktan 1966, 111; Scherzer 1873, 37–39.

45. Karpat (1983) estimates that during the second half of the nineteenth century the population of the Ottoman Empire grew at an average rate of 1%. Issawi (1980) estimates this percentage as 0.64 for the Muslims and 0.88 for non-Muslims (p. 18). For the population of İzmir in various years, see Issawi 1980, 34; Farley 1862, 81; Scherzer 1873, 41; Cuinet 1889, 440; Karpat 1978, 258; Frangakis 1984; Goffman 1985.

46. Special stones were brought from Naples to be used in some of these constructions. See Kıray 1972, 51–52. For the details of the quay project, see Georgiades 1885, 154–158.

47. FO 195/797: 77, 30 May 1864.

48. Ubicini 1856, 249–250; Scherzer 1873, 67–68.

49. See Issawi 1980, 18; Pamuk 1984, 191; Clogg 1982, 195.

50. Total population of the coastal area in the immediate vicinity of İzmir and the main towns of the interior (i.e., including İzmir, Çeşme, Kuşadası, Foça, Bergama, Kasaba, Aydın, Manisa Denizli, and Muğla) amounted to less than 30% of the total province of the Aydın province in 1884. See Cuinet 1892, passim.

51. On this point see Keyder 1981.

52. It is further indicative of the changing relational network in the region that the seat of provincial government was moved from Aydın to İzmir in 1851.

53. For example, "peasants obtained a lot of money from the sale of their product to the Allied Forces during the [Crimean] War." FO 78/1302: 313–325, 18 February 1857.

54. In 1842, according to Consul Sandison, around Bursa "outside of the Turkish population, the condition of the peasantry was often exhibiting substance and generally self sufficiency for subsistence." FO 78/490: 238–247, 19 February 1842.

55. Great Britain, *Sessional Papers,* 1867–1868, LXVIII: 231; Kurmuş 1974, 67; Kıray 1972, 13–15.

56. Scherzer 1873, 72. For cost of transportation, see Kurmuş 1974, 46.

57. At one point, both the railway company and the caravan owners tried to hire bandits to disrupt each other's business. See Kıray 1972, 14.

58. In 1855, in one of his reports from Bursa, Consul Sandison made the following remarks: "There ought to have been a considerable surplus for export from the district and the producers would have had the fair benefit of the revenue instead of so much of it being absorbed by camel drivers, a sluggish and unworthy set of people much identified with their beasts of burden, and whose gains contribute little or nothing to reproductive agriculture." FO 78/1209: 45.

59. See Boratav et al. 1985, 390, 402; also, Issawi 1980, 37–43.

60. There is evidence to suggest that wage employment in small- and middle-sized holdings was quite prevalent. See Pamuk 1984, 88–94.

61. In 1841, an unskilled worker in agriculture was making 3kr. (6.5d.)/day. Prices of some of the necessities were: mutton = 2d./lb.; flour = 1.5d./lb. [FO 78/441: 240-245, 28 January 1841]. In 1864, an unskilled agricultural worker could make as much as 9.75 kr. (21d)/day; prices of the necessities were: mutton = 3.5-5d./lb.; flour = 3d./lb.; beef = 2-2.5d./lb.; butter = 9-12d./lb.; turkeys = 2s.8d.-4s.6d. each; fowls = 6-11d. each [FO 78/1876: 58]. See also Boratav et al. 1985; and Issawi 1980.

62. Sussintzki 1966, 121.

63. See Chapman 1977, 35-41.

64. The Estate of E. Henry, FO 626/1: File 19, (1860-61).

65. Joint estates of Racine and Bedros, IMS-III: 5 (1853/54); Estate of Baltaci Manolaki, IMS, I: 4 (1853/54); The Estate of Bolaniye, IMS, XXIII: 114 (1867); etc.

66. The Estate of E. Henry, FO 626/1: file 19 (1860-61); The Estate of Bolaniye, IMS, XXIII: 114 (1867).

67. FO 78/1831: 160, 2 August 1864.

68. FO 195/299: 217-232, 10 January 1848.

69. Ali 1976, 18.

70. Barsoumian 1982, 173.

71. It should be noted that the church hierarchy and the local communities did not always concur; in fact, in the course of the nineteenth century, they increasingly disagreed more than they agreed on many issues. These divisions became especially pronounced and pertinent during the nationalist uprisings in the Balkans, which were as much against the dominant circles within the Orthodox church as they were against the Ottoman overrule. See Karpat 1982. Similar divisions appeared in other non-Muslim communities as well. For the Armenians, see Barsoumian 1982.

72. The state of different neighborhoods can be assessed from the effects of the cholera epidemic in 1865, when in one month between June and July, 232 people died in İzmir; of these, 167 were Jewish, 38 Greek, 10 Turk, 6 Armenian, 8 Catholic, 3 Protestant; ". . . to which must be added 73 deaths among Jews from various causes the bodies being found in deserted houses." FO 78/1888: 231, 21 July 1865. For Senior's impressions of İzmir's suburbs, see 1859, 204-205; for a description of the Jewish neighborhood of İzmir, see Dumont 1982.

73. For example, see İnalcık 1969, 110-113; Jennings 1973.

74. Bağış 1983, 59-60; Bilget 1949, 65.

75. Not until 1881 did a muslim merchant in İzmir organize an export trade, and then with an Armenian partner. Bilget 1949, 12-65.

76. For example, in 1845, the governor forced the corporation of bakers in Ödemiş to purchase 5,000 kilos of wheat from him at 10kr/kilo, whereas the market price was 6.5 kr/kilo. FO 195/241: 213-218, 15 April 1845.

77. In 1846, the governor of Karahisar imposed a monopoly on opium, which caused a sharp decline in exports. See Appendix, Table A.6. Also, FO 78/701: 64-71, 83, 31 March 1847, 9 April 1847; FO 195/299: 70-72, 203-210, 9 April 1847, 14 December 1847.

78. Veinstein 1976, 74-75.

79. Veinstein 1976, 76.

80. FO 195/241: 213-218, 15 April 1845. Also in Issawi 1980, 351.

81. In 1857, N. Senior was told in İzmir, "No one ever heard of a Turkish house of business or of a Turkish banker, or merchant, or manufacture. . . . The only considerable enterprise in which he ever engages is the farming, some branch of public revenue. . . . Whenever a Turk borrows, lender is a Greek, whenever a Turk sells the purchaser is a Greek . . . and it is seldom that a Turk [buys] without soon having to sell" (1859, 211-214).

82. Replies to the questionnaire on the general conditions of Christians in Turkey, 1860, FO 78/1533: 273-276, 281-283, 28 July 1860.

83. In one instance, a large estate was divided by the İzmir court into 128 shares, each valued at about 500 kr. IMS, I:33 (1853). For various vakıfs, I:35 (1857); I:41 (1862); III:4 (1853/54). For a discussion of vakıf property along these lines, see Ülgener 1981, 171.

84. As in IMS, I:3 (1850); IMS, I:33 (1845).

85. For a description of the various aspects of ethnic division of labor in the Ottoman Empire, see Sussintzki 1966, 118; Ubicini 1856a, 225-228, 310-318; Dumont 1982, 218-219; Clogg 1982, 196; Rosenthal 1982, 372.

86. See the classical description by Ubicini 1856, 339-340; about "deindustrialization," see Kurmuş 1981; Pamuk 1984, 103-125. The most notable exception to this general trend was the carpet manufacturing which, for the most part, employed Muslims and remained viable throughout the nineteenth century. See Quataert 1986.

CHAPTER 5

1. There is some skepticism among economic historians regarding the appropriateness of characterizing these years as those of "depression" or "crisis." For

a summary of discussion, see Saul 1969; Hanson 1980, 90–92. Two aspects of these decades, however, are beyond dispute: first, that they involved the displacement of Britain form its hegemonic position in the world economy; second, that they marked the end of the inflationary trends of the previous era. For price trends and other economic indicators of a global contraction, see Lewis 1978; Hanson 1980, 14–15; Bairoch 1973, 25. Also see Mitchell 1981, 773; Arrighi 1978a.

2. Saul 1969, 30–34.

3. See Landes 1966, 472ff.

4. See Polanyi 1957, 9–15; Arrighi 1978, 116–121.

5. On the relationship between capital movements and state policies during the last quarter of the nineteenth century, see Feis 1930, 61, 88–89, 134, 156–157, 162–169; see also Viner 1928.

6. Arrighi 1978, 126–131; also, Landes 1966, 554–556ff.

7. Polanyi 1957, Chap. 1; Arrighi 1978, 69–71.

8. See Findley 1980, 66–68; 224ff.

9. Shaw 1975; Akarlı 1976.

10. Akarlı 1976.

11. Lewis 1976, 181–194.

12. Eldem 1970.

13. Quataert 1973.

14. The first being in the wake of the Napoleonic Wars; see Chapter three.

15. Blaisdell (1966), which was originally published in 1929, remains the best treatise on PDA. Also see Du Velay 1978, 299–360; Morawitz 1979, 184–304; Feis 1930, 332–341. For a summary, see Owen 1981, 192–200.

16. On Régie, see the sources cited in n. 15 above. Also see Quataert 1983, 13–40; Mutluçağ 1967.

17. Blaisdell 1966, 150–151; Parvus 1977, 71–74.

18. Issawi 1980, 77.

19. See Blaisdell 1966, 151–152.

20. Blaisdell 1966, 235–237; Feis 1930, 339–341.

21. Blaisdell 1966, 6–7.

22. Blaisdell 1966, 118; also see Parvus 1977, 75.

23. Parvus 1977, 77.

24. Interestingly enough, over 90% of the PDA's employees were Ottoman Muslims. (Blaisdell 1966, 118.)

25. See Chapter three.

26. Pamuk 1984a, 111–112.

27. See Quataert 1983, 18–19. See also Mutluçağ 1967.

28. Eldem 1970, 133–134.

29. Aybar 1939, 44, 76.

30. Issawi 1980, 77.

31. See Table 2; also, see Keyder 1983.

32. Pamuk 1984a, 113; Cottrell 1975, 45–46.

33. Pamuk 1984a, 110.

34. For a comprehensive account, see Toprak 1982; see also Ahmad 1980.

CHAPTER 6

1. Four recent studies reach parallel conclusions, indicating the existence of similar developments and transformations in other parts of the empire. Fawaz (1983), in comparing Beirut with Alexandria, attributes the success of the former to the preponderance of local merchants in this city's relations with the world markets. Owen (1981) concludes that the economic growth of the nineteenth century involved an increase in local incomes in the Middle East. Davis (1983) rejects the arguments that posit a harmony of interests between the domestic bourgeoisie in Egypt and foreign bourgeoisies. Finally, Quataert (1983) describes how local networks mobilized to resist the penetration of the Régie in Anatolia.

2. On "historical alternatives," see Weber 1949.

APPENDIX

1. For a comprehensive presentation of weights and measures, see İnalcık 1983a; see also Pyle 1977; Toprak 1983.

2. FO 78/1533: 190, 31 March 1860; FO 78/1760: 256–258, 21 November 1863.

3. İnalcık 1983a, 337; Pyle 1977.

4. İnalcık 1983a, 335.

5. Kula 1986, Chaps. 14–17.

6. The works by the following were especially helpful: Scherzer (1873), who was the Austria-Hungarian Consul in the 1860s and the 1870s; Rougon (1892), who was the French Consul during the same years; and Georgiades (1885), who was a merchant in İzmir.

Bibliography

UNPUBLISHED SOURCES

I. *Great Britain,* Public Record Office, London
   1. Board of Customs and Excise
      Customs 4. *Ledgers of Imports,* 1840–1876
   2. Board of Trade
      BT 1/569. *Petition for the Grant of a Charter of Incorporation to a Proposed Bank in Izmir,* 1843.
   3. Foreign Office
      FO 78. *General Correspondence.* Original Dispatches and Reports from British consular representatives in the Ottoman Empire; Miscellaneous Correspondence with individuals, and drafts or copies of letters sent from Foreign Office, 1840–1876.
      FO 195. *Consular Archives,* İzmir and Bursa.
      FO 626. *Smyrna Consular Court.*
II. *Turkey,* Archeological Museum, İzmir.
    Records of the Ottoman Court in İzmir.
    IMS, I–XXXI. Court Records, 1854–1875.

OFFICIAL PUBLICATIONS

Great Britain, Parliament, House of Commons, *Accounts and Papers, Annual Statement of Trade,* 1854–1873.

159

Great Britain, Parliament, House of Commons, *Sessional Papers*, 1854–1876.

SECONDARY SOURCES

Abdul Rahman, A., and Y. Nagata. 1977. "The İltizam System in Egypt and Turkey." *Journal of Asian and African Studies* XIV:169–94.

Abou-el-Haj, Rifa'at Ali. 1974. "Ottoman Attitudes Toward Peace Making: The Karlowitz Case." *Der Islam* LI:131–37.

Ahmad, Feroz. 1980. "Vanguard of Nascent Bourgeoisie: The Social and Economic Policy of Young Turks, 1980–1918." In O. Okyar and H. İnalcık, eds., *Türkiye'nin Sosyal ve Ekonomik Tarihi, 1071–1920*, 329–50. Ankara: Meteksan.

———. 1984. "The State Intervention in Turkey." *Turcica* XVI:51–64.

Akarlı, Engin D. 1976. "The Problems of External Pressures, Power Struggles and Budgetary Deficits in Ottoman Politics under Abdülhamid II (1876–1909). Unpublished Ph.D. Dissertation, Princeton, University.

Akbal, Fazıla. 1951. "1831 Tarihinde Osmanlı İmparatorluğunda İdari Taksimat ve Nüfus." *Belleten* XV:60, Ekim, 617–28.

Aktan, Reşat. 1966. "Agricultural Policy of Turkey." In C. Issawi, ed., *The Economic History of the Middle East, 1800–1914*, 108–13. Chicago and London: University of Chicago Press.

Ali. 1976. *İstanbul'da Elli Yıllık Önemli Olaylar*. İstanbul: Sander.

Amin, Samir. 1976. *Unequal Development*. New York: Monthly Review Press.

Anderson, M. S. 1966. *The Eastern Question*. London and New York: St. Martin's Press.

Anderson, Olive. 1961. "Economic Warfare in the Crimean War." *Economic History Review*, Second Series, XIV, 1, 34–47.

———. 1964. "Great Britain and the Beginnings of the Ottoman Public Debt, 1854–55." *The Historical Journal* VII, 1:47–63.

Arrighi, Giovanni. 1978. *The Geometry of Imperialism*. London: New Left Books.

_____. 1978a. "Towards a Theory of Capitalist Crisis." *New Left Review* 111 (Sept-Oct.):3–24.

_____, and Jessica Drangel. 1986. "The Stratification of the World Economy: An Exploration of the Semiperipheral Zone." *Review* X, 1 (Summer): 9–74.

Ashworth, William. 1962. *A Short History of the International Economy Since 1850.* London: Longman.

Aybar, Celal. 1939. *Osmanlı İmparatorluğunun Ticaret Muvazenesi 1878–1913.* Ankara: Başvekalet İstatistik Enstitüsü.

Aymard, Maurice. 1966. *Venise, Raguse et le commerce du blé pendant la seconde moitié du XVIe siècle.* Paris: École Pratique des Hautes Etudes.

Baer, Gabriel. 1970. "Guilds in the Middle Eastern History." In M. A. Cook, ed., *Studies in the Economic History of the Middle East,* 11–30. London: Oxford University Press.

_____. 1970a. "The Administrative Economic and Social Functions of Turkish Guilds," *International Journal of Middle East Studies* I:28–50.

Bağış, Ali İhsan. 1983. *Osmanlı Ticaretinde Gayri Müslimler.* Ankara: Turhan Kitabevi.

Bailey, Frank Edgar. 1970. *British Policy and the Turkish Reform Movement: A Study in Anglo-Turkish Relations, 1826–1853.* New York: Howard Fertig.

Bairoch, Paul. 1973. "European Foreign Trade in the XIX Century: The development of the Value and Volume of Exports (Preliminary Results)." *Journal of European Economic History* II (Spring):5–36.

_____. 1974. "Geographical Structure and Trade Balance of European Foreign Trade from 1800 to 1970." *Journal of European Economic History* III (Winter):557–608.

Barkan, Ömer Lütfi. 1942. "Osmanlı İmparatorluğunda Bir İskân ve Kolonizasyon Metodu Olarak Vakıflar ve Temlikler." *Vakıflar Dergisi* II:279–365.

_____. 1949-1954. "Osmanlı İmparatorluğunda Bir İskân ve Kolonizasyon Metodu Olarak Sürgünler." *Istanbul Üniversitesi İktisat Fakültesi Mecmuası* XI:524–569; XIII:56–79; XIV:209–237.

————. 1957. "Essai sur les donnes statistique des registres de recensment dans l'Empire Ottomane aux XVe et XVIe siècles." *Journal of the Economic and Social History of the Orient* I:1, 9–36.

————. 1975. "The Price Revolution of the 16th Century." *International Journal of Middle-East Studies* VI, (Jan.):3–28.

————. 1980. *Türkiye'de Toprak Meselesi. Toplu Eserleri: 1,* İstanbul: Gözlem.

Barsoumian, Hagop. 1982. "The Dual Role of the Armenian Amira Class within the Ottoman Government and the Armenian Millet (1750–1850)." In B. Braude and B. Lewis, eds., *Christians and Jews in the Ottoman Empire: The Functioning of a Plural Society I, The Central Lands,* 171–84. New York and London: Holmes and Meier.

Berend, I. T., and Gy. Ranki. 1982. *The European Periphery and Industrialization 1780–1914.* Cambridge: Cambridge University Press.

Bilget, Adnan. 1949. *Son Yüzyılda İzmir.* İzmir: Meşhet Basımevi.

Blaisdell, Donald C. 1966. *European Financial Control in the Ottoman Empire: A Study of the Establishment, Activities, and Significance of the Administration of the Ottoman Public Debt.* New York: AM-Press.

Bodman, Herbert, Jr. 1963. *Political Factions in Aleppo, 1760–1826.* Chapel Hill: The University of North Carolina Press.

Boratav, Korkut, Gündüz Ökçün, Şevket Pamuk. 1985. "Ottoman Wages and the World Economy, 1839–1913." *Review* VIII, 3 (Winter):379–406.

Born, Erich. 1983. *International Banking.* Warwickshire: Berg.

Braude, Benjamin. 1979. "International Competition and Domestic Cloth in the Ottoman Empire, 1500–1650: A Study on Underdevelopment." *Review* II, 3 (Winter):937–51.

Braudel, Fernand. 1972. *The Mediterranean and the Mediterranean World in the Age of Philip II* Vol. I. London: Fontana.

————. 1973. *The Mediterranean and the Mediterranean World in the Age of Philip II,* Vol. II. New York: Harper and Row.

————. 1984. *The Perspective of the World, Civilization and Capitalism, 15–18th Century,* III. New York: Harper and Row.

_____, and Frank Spooner. 1967. "Prices in Europe from 1450 to 1750." In *Cambridge Economic History of Europe, IV*, E. E. Rich and C. H. Wilson, eds., *The Economy of Expanding Europe in the 16th and 17th Centuries*, 374-486. London: Cambridge University Press.

Busch-Zantner, R. 1938. *Agrarverfassung Gesellschaft und Sidelung in Sudosteuropa*. Leipzig: O. Harrassowitz.

Çadırcı, Musa. 1980. "II. Mahmut Döneminde (1808-1839) Avrupa ve Hayriye Tüccarları." O. Okyar and H. İnalcık, eds., *Türkiye'nin Sosyal ve Ekonomik Tarihi 1071-1920*, 237-41. Ankara: Meteksan.

Cevdet Paşa. 1953. *Tezâkir*, 1-12. Ankara: Türk Tarih Kurumu.

Cezar, Yavuz. 1986. *Osmanlı Maliyesinde Bunalım ve Değişim Dönemi*. İstanbul: Alan Yayıncılık.

Chapman, S. 1977. "The International Houses: The Continental Contribution to British Commerce, 1800-1860." *Journal of the European Economic History* VI, 1 (Spring):5-48.

Chirot, Daniel. 1976. *Social Change in a Peripheral Society: The Creation of a Balkan Colony*. New York: Academic Press.

Church, R. A. 1979. *The Great Victorian Boom, 1850-1873*. London: Macmillan.

Çizakça, Murat. 1980. "Price History and the Bursa Silk Industry, A Study in Ottoman Industrial Decline, 1550-1650," *Journal of Economic History* XL, 3 (September):533-550.

Clapham, J. H. 1968. *The Economic Development of France and Germany*, fourth ed. Cambridge: Cambridge University Press.

Clark, Edward C. 1974. "The Ottoman Industrial Revolution," *International Journal of Middle East Studies* V:65-76.

Clogg, Richard ed.. 1976. *The Movement for Greek Independence: A Collection of Documents*. New York: Barnes & Noble.

_____. 1981. "The Greek Mercantile Bourgeoisie Progressive or Reactionary?" In R. Clogg, ed., *Balkan Society in the Age of Greek Independence*, 85-110. London: Macmillan.

_____. 1982. "The Greek Millet in the Ottoman Empire." In B. Braude abd B. Lewis, eds., *Christians and Jews in the Ottoman Empire: The*

Functioning of a Plural Society, I, The Central Lands, 185–207. New York and London: Holmes & Meier.

Cole, W. A., and Phyllis Deane. 1966. "The Growth of National Incomes." In *The Cambridge Economic History of Europe,* VI, H. J. Habakkuk and M. Postan, eds., *The Industrial Revolutions and After: Incomes, Population and Technological Change (1),* 1–55. Cambridge: Cambridge University Press.

Cook, M. A. 1972. *Population Pressure in Rural Anatolia 1450–1600.* London: Oxford University Press.

Cottrell, P. 1975. *British Overseas Investment in the Nineteenth Century.* London: Macmillan.

Cuinet, Vital. 1892. *LaTurquie d'Asie, Géographie administrative statistique descriptive et raisonnée de chaque province de l'Asie Mineure, III: Basra, İzmir, Biga.* Paris: E. Leroux.

Dames Longworth. 1921. "The Portuguese and the Turks in the Indian Ocean in the Sixteenth Century." *Journal of the Royal Asiatic Society,* 1–28.

Davis, Eric. 1983. *Challenging Colonialism: Bank Misr and Egyptian Industrialization, 1920–1941.* Princeton: Princeton University Press.

Davis, Ralph. 1979. *The Industrial Revolution and British Overseas Trade.* Leicester, Leicester University Press.

Davison, Roderick. 1963. *Reform in the Ottoman Empire.* Princeton: Princeton University Press.

———. 1980. "The First Ottoman Experiment with Paper Money." In O. Okyar and H. İnalcık, eds., *Türkiyenin Sosyal ve Ekonomik Tarihi, 1071–1920,* 243–51. Ankara: Meteksan.

Devereux, Robert. 1963. *The First Ottoman Constitutional Period.* Baltimore: Johns Hopkins Press.

Dovring, Folke. 1966. "The Transformation of European Agriculture." In *The Cambridge Economic History of Europe,* Vol. VI, H. J. Habakkuk and M. Postan, eds., *The Industrial Revolutions and After: Incomes, Population and Technological Change,* II, 603–72. Cambridge: Cambridge University Press.

Dumont, Paul. 1982. "Jewish Communities in Turkey during the Last Decades of the Nineteenth Century in the Light of the Archives of the Alliance Israélite Universelle." In B. Braude and B. Lewis, eds., *Christians and Jews in the Ottoman Empire: Functioning of a Plural Society*, I, *Central Lands*, 209-42. New York and London: Holmes and Meier.

Du Velay, A. 1978. *Türkiye Maliye Tarihi*. Ankara: Maliye Bakanlığı Tetkik Kurulu. [Original: *Essai sur l'histoire financière de la Turquie depuis le règne du Sultan Mahmoud II jusqou à nos jours*. Paris: A. Rousseau, 1903.]

Eldem, Vedat. 1970. *Osmanlı İmparatorluğunun İktisadi Şartları Hakkında Bir Tetkik*. Ankara: T. İş Bankası Kültür Yayınları.

Emmanuel, Arghiri. 1972. "White Settler Colonialism and the Myth of Investment Imperialism." *New Left Review* 73 (May-June):35-57.

Fairlie, Susan. 1964. "Dyestuffs in the Eighteenth Century," *Economic History Review*, 2nd series, XVII, 488-510.

———. 1969. "The Corn Laws and British Wheat Production, 1829-76." *Economic History Review*, 2nd series, XXII, 1 (April):88-113.

Farley, James Lewis. 1862. *The Resources of Turkey Considered with Special Reference to the Profitable Investment of Capital in the Ottoman Empire*. London: Longman, Green, Longman and Roberts.

Faroqhi, Suraiya. 1977. "Rural Society in Anatolia and the Balkans during the Sixteenth Century (I)" *Turcica* IX/1:161-95.

———. 1979. "Rural Society in Anatolia and the Balkans during the Sixteenth Century (II)" *Turcica* XI:103-53.

———. 1979a. "Sixteenth Century Periodic Markets in Various Anatolian Sancaks: İçel, Hamid, Karahisar-ı Sahib, Kütahya, Aydın, Menteşe." *Journal of the Economic and Social History of the Orient* XXII, 1 (Jan.):32-80.

———. 1984. *Towns and Townsmen in Ottoman Anatolia, 1520-1650*. Cambridge: Cambridge University Press.

———. 1986. "The Venetian Presence in the Ottoman Empire, 1600-1630." *The Journal of European Economic History* XV, 4 (Fall):345-84.

Fawaz, Leila. 1983. *Merchants and Migrants in Nineteenth Century Beirut*. Cambridge: Harvard University Press.

Feis, Herbert. 1930. *Europe, The World's Banker 1870–1914.* New Haven: Yale University Press.

Findley, Carter V. 1980. *Bureaucratic Reform in the Ottoman Empire: The Sublime Porte, 1789–1922.* Princeton: Princeton University Press.

Fisher, Charles A. 1966. "The Changing Dimensions of Europe." *Journal of Contemporary History* I, 3 (July) 3–20.

Fleischer, Cornell. 1986. *Bureaucrat and Intellectual in the Ottoman Empire.* Princeton: Princeton University Press.

Frangakis, Elena. 1984. "The Commerce of İzmir in the Eighteenth Century, 1695–1820." Unpublished Ph.D. Dissertation, King's College, London University.

Frank, Andre Gunder. 1978. *Dependent Accumulation and Underdevelopment.* New York: Monthly Review Press.

Friedmann, Harriet. 1978. "World Market, State and Family Farm: Social Bases of Household Production in the Era of Wage Labor." *Comparative Studies in Society and History* XX, 4 (Oct.) 545–86.

Gallagher, John, and R. Robinson. 1953. "The Imperialism of Free Trade." *Economic History Review*, 2nd series, VI, 1, 1–15.

Gandev, Christo. 1960. "L'apparition des rapports capitalistes dans l'économie rurale de la Bulgarie du nord-ouest au cours du XVIIIe siècle." *Études Historiques* I:207–20.

Genç, Mehmet. 1984. "Osmanlı Ekonomisi ve Savaş." *Yapıt*, 4, Nisan-Mayıs, 52–61; 5, Haziran-Temmuz, 86–93.

Georgiades, Demetrios. 1885. *Smyrne et l'Asie Mineure au point de vue économique et commercial.* Paris: Impr. Chaix.

Gerber, Haim. 1987. *The Social Origins of the Modern Middle East.* Boulder: Lynne Rienner.

Girard, L. 1966. "Transport." In *The Cambridge Economic History of Europe*, Vol. VI, H. J. Habakkuk and M. Postan, eds., *The Industrial Revolutions and After: Incomes, Population and Technological Change* (1). Cambridge: The University Press.

Glass, D. V., and E. Grebenik. 1966. "World Population, 1800–1950." In *The Cambridge Economic History of Europe*, Vol. VI, H. J.

Habakkuk and M. Postan, eds., *The Industrial Revolutions and After: Incomes, Population and Technological Change* (1). Cambridge: The University Press.

Goffman, Daniel. 1985. *İzmir as a Commercial Center: The Impact of Western Trade on an Ottoman Porte, 1570–1650.* Unpublished Ph.D. Dissertation, University of Chicago.

Gordon, L. James. 1932. *American Relations with Turkey, 1830–1930, an Economic Interpretation.* Philadelphia: University of Pennsylvania Press.

Gould, Andrew. 1976. "Lords or Bandits? The Derebeys of Cilicia." *International Journal of Middle East Studies* VII:4, 485–506.

Gökbilgin, Tayyib. 1967. "Tanzimat Hareketinin Osmanlı Müesseselerine ve Teşkilatına Etkileri." *Belleten* XXXI:93–111.

Güçer, Lütfü. 1964. *XVI-XVII Asırlarda Osmanlı İmparatorluğunda Hububat Meselesi ve Hububattan Alınan Vergiler.* İstanbul: Sermet Matbaası.

_____. 1980. "Grain Supply of İstanbul in the Eighteenth Century." In C. Issawi, *The Economic History of Turkey, 1800–1914*, 24–33. Chicago: The University of Chicago Press.

Güran, Tevfik. n.d. "Osmanlı Tarım Ekonomisine Giriş, 1840–1910." Unpublished manuscript.

Haddad, William, and William Ochsenwald, eds. 1977. *Nationalism in a Nonnational State.* Columbus: Ohio State University Press.

Hanson, John R. 1980. *Trade in Transition, Exports from the Third World, 1840–1900.* New York: Academic Press.

Hess, Andrew. 1970. "The Evolution of the Ottoman Seaborne Empire in the Age of the Oceanic Discoveries, 1453–1525." *American Historical Review* LXXV, 7 (Dec.):1892–1919.

Hobsbawm, Eric. 1962. *The Age of Revolution.* New York: Mentor.

_____. 1968. *Industry and Empire.* Harmondsworth: Penguin.

_____. 1979. *The Age of Capital 1848–1975.* New York: Mentor.

Hopkins, Terence K. 1979. "The Study of the Capitalist World Economy: Some Introductory Considerations." In W. L. Goldfrank, ed., *The World System of Capitalism, Past and Present.* Beverly Hills: Sage.

————, and Immanuel Wallerstein. 1977. "Patterns of Development of the Modern World System." *Review* I, 2 (Fall):111–45.

————, and Immanuel Wallerstein. 1981. "Structural Transformations of the World Economy." In R. Rubinson, ed., *Dynamics of World Development*, 233–261. Beverly Hills: Sage.

Hourani, Albert. 1968. "Ottoman Reform and the Politics of Notables." In W. Polk and R. Chanbers, eds., *Beginnings of Modernization in the Middle East: The Nineteenth Century*, 41–68. Chicago: The University of Chicago Press.

Hurewitz, J. C. 1961. "The Europeanization of Ottoman Diplomacy: The Conversion from Unilateralism to Reciprocity in the Nineteenth Century." *Belleten* XXV, 99, Temmuz, 455–66.

————. 1975. *The Middle East and North Africa in World Politics: A Documentary Record, I: European Expansion 1535–1914*, 2nd ed. New Haven: Yale University Press.

Imlah, Albert Henry. 1958. *Economic Elements in the Pax-Britannica*. Cambridge: Harvard University Press.

İnalcık, Halil. 1954. "Ottoman Methods of Conquest." *Studia Islamica* II:103–129.

————. 1960. "Bursa and the Commerce of the Levant," *Journal of Economic and Social History of the Orient* III:2, 131–47.

————. 1964a. "Sened-i İttifak ve Gülhane Hatt-ı Hümayunu," *Belleten* XXVIII:112, 603–621.

————. 1964b. "Tanzimatın Uygulanması ve Sosyal Tepkileri." *Belleten* XXVIII:112, 623–690.

————. 1969. "Capital Formation in the Ottoman Empire." *The Journal of Economic History* XXIX, 1 (March):97–140.

————. 1971. "İmtiyazat: The Ottoman Empire," *Encyclopedia of Islam*, 2nd ed., III, 1179–1189. Leiden: E. J. Brill.

————. 1973. *The Ottoman Empire: The Classical Age, 1300–1600.* New York: Praeger.

————. 1975. "Kanun." *Encyclopedia of Islam*, 2nd ed., IV, 556–62. Leiden: E. J. Brill.

_____. 1975a. "Kanunname." *Encyclopedia of Islam,* 2nd ed., IV, 562–66. Leiden: E. J. Brill.

_____. 1977. "Centralization, Decentralization in Ottoman Administration." In T. Naff and R. Owen, eds., *Studies in Eighteenth Century Islamic History,* 27–52. Carbondale: Southern Illinois University Press.

_____. 1978. "The Ottoman Decline and Its Effects Upon the Reaya." In *The Ottoman Empire: Conquest, Organization and Economy,* 338–354. London: Variorum Reprints.

_____. 1980. "Osmanlı Pamuklu Pazarı, Hindistan ve İngiltere: Pazar Rekabetinde Emek Maliyetinin Rolü." *ODTÜ Gelişme Dergisi/METU Studies in Development,* 1979/1980, 1–65.

_____. 1980a. "Military and Fiscal Transformation in the Ottoman Empire, 1600–1700." *Archivum Ottomanicum* VI:283–337.

_____. 1983. "The Emergence of Big Farms, Çiftliks: State, Landlords and Tenants." In J. L. Bacqué-Grammont et P. Dumont, eds., *Contributions à l'Histoire Économique et Sociale de l'Empire Ottoman,* 105–26. Leuven: Ed. Peeters, 1983.

_____. 1983a. "Introduction to Ottoman Metrology." *Turcica* XV:311–48.

Iseminger, Gordon L. 1968. "The Old Turkish Hands: The British Levantine Consuls, 1856–1876." *Middle East Journal* XXII, 3 (Summer):297–316.

Işıksal, Cavide. 1968. "Türkiye'de İlk Bankacılık Hareketi ve Osmanlı Bankasının Kurulması." *Belgelerle Türk Tarihi Dergisi,* I, 10, Temmuz, 72–79.

Islamoğlu, Huri and Çağlar Keyder. 1977. "Agenda for Ottoman History." *Review* I, 1 (Summer):31–55.

_____, and Suraiya Faroqhi. 1979. "Crop Patterns and Agricultural Trends in Sixteenth Century Anatolia." *Review* II, 2 (Winter):401–36.

Issawi, Charles (ed. with Introductions). 1966. *The Economic History of the Middle East 1800–1914.* Chicago and London: The University of Chicago Press.

_____. 1970. "The Decline of Middle-Eastern Trade, 1100–1850." In D. S. Richards, ed., *Islam and the Trade of Asia,* 245–66. Oxford: Oxford University Press.

_____. 1977. "Population and Resources in the Ottoman Empire and Iran." In T. Naff and R. Owen, eds., *Studies in the Eighteenth Century Islamic History*, 152-54. Carbondale: Southern Illinois University Press.

_____. 1980. *The Economic History of Turkey: 1800-1914*. Chicago: The University of Chicago Press.

_____. 1982. "The Transformation and the Economic Position of the Millets in the 19th Century." In B. Braude and B. Lewis, eds., *Christians and Jews in the Ottoman Empire*, I, 261-85. New York and London: Holmes & Meier.

Itzkowitz, Norman. 1980. *Ottoman Empire and Islamic Tradition*. Chicago and London: University of Chicago Press.

Jelavich, Charles and Barbara. 1977. *The Establishment of the Balkan National States: 1804-1920*. Seattle: University of Washington Press.

Jenks, Leland H. 1973. *The Migration of British Capital to 1875*. New York: Barnes and Noble.

Jennings, Ronald C. 1973. "Loans and Credit in Early 17th c. Ottoman Judicial Records." *Journal of the Economic and Social History of the Orient* XVI:168-216.

Kançal, Salgur. 1983. "La conquête du marché interne par le capitalisme industriel concurrentiel (1838-1881)." In J. L. Bacqué-Grammont and Paul Dumont, eds., *Économie et sociétiés dans l'Empire Ottoman*, 355-409. Paris: Éditions du Centre National de la Recherche Scientifique.

Karidis, Viron. 1981. "A Greek Mercantile Paroikia: Odessa: 1774-1829." In R. Clogg, ed., *Balkan Society in the Age of Greek Independence*, 111-36. London: Macmillan.

Karpat, Kemal. 1973. *An Inquiry into the Social Foundations of Nationalism in the Ottoman State*. Princeton: The Woodrow Wilson School, Princeton University.

_____. 1978. "Ottoman Population Records and the Census of 1881/82-1893." *International Journal of Middle East Studies* IX:237-74.

_____. 1982. "Millets and Nationality: The Roots of the Incongruity of Nation and State in the Post-Ottoman Era." In B. Braude and B.

Lewis, eds., *Christians and Jews in the Ottoman Empire: The Functioning of a Plural Society,* I, *The Central Lands,* 141-69. New York and London: Holmes and Meier.

———. 1983. "The Ottoman Demography in the Nineteenth Century: Sources, Concepts, Methods." In J. L. Bacque-Grammont and Paul Dumont, eds., *Economie et Societes dans l'Empire Ottoman,* 207-18. Paris: Éditions du Centre National de la Recherche Scientifique.

———. 1985. *Ottoman Population 1830-1914: Demographic and Social Characteristics.* Madison: University of Wisconsin Press.

Kasaba, Reşat. 1985. "Geç Dönem Osmanlı Toplumsal Tarihi İçin Kaynak Olarak Mahkeme Sicilleri." *Tarih ve Toplum,* 14, Şubat, 49-53.

———. 1986. *Peripheralization of the Ottoman Empire.* Unpublished Ph.D. Dissertation, State University of New York at Binghamton.

Kazgan, Haydar. 1977. "Osmanlı Kaynaklarına Göre İstanbuldaki Esham ve Tahvilat Borsası ve Borsa Oyunları." *Toplum ve Bilim,* 2, Yaz, 157-64.

Keyder, Çağlar. 1981. "Proto-Industrialization and the Periphery: A Marxist Perspective." *The Insurgent Sociologist* X, 3 (Winter):51-57.

———. 1983. "Small Peasant Ownership in Turkey: Historical Formation and Present Structure." *Review* VII, 1 (Summer):53-107.

———. 1983a. "The Cycle of Sharecropping and the Consolidation of Small Peasant Ownership in Turkey." *The Journal of Peasant Studies* X, 2-3 (Jan/April):130-45.

Kıray, Mübeccel Belik. 1972. *Örgülteşemeyen Kent: İzmirde İş Hayatının Yapısı ve Yerleşme Düzeni.* Ankara: Türk Sosyal Bilimler Derneği.

Kondratieff, N. D. 1979. "The Long Waves in Economic Life." *Review* II, 4 (Spring):519-62.

Kortepeter, Carl M. 1966. "Ottoman Imperial Policy and the Economy of the Black Sea Region in the 16th Century." *Journal of the American Oriental Society* LXXXVI:86-113.

Köymen, Oya. 1971. "The Advent and Consequences of Free Trade in the Ottoman Empire." *Etudes Balkaniques,* 2.

Kunt, Metin. 1983. *The Sultan's Servants, the Transformation of Ottoman Provincial Government 1550–1650.* New York: Columbia University Press.

Kurmus, Orhan. 1974. *Emperyalizmin Türkiye'ye Girişi.* İstanbul: Bilim Yayinları.

————. 1981. "Some Aspects of Handicraft and Industrial Production in Ottoman Anatolia, 1800–1915." *Asian and African Studies* XV, 1 (March) 85–101.

————. 1987. "The Cotton Famine and Its Effects on the Ottoman Empire." In H. İslamoğlu-İnan ed. *The Ottoman Empire and the World Economy,* 160–169. Cambridge: Cabmridge University Press.

Kütükoğlu, Mübahat S. 1976. *Osmanlı-İngiliz İktisadi Münasebetleri, II, 1838–1850.* Istanbul: Edebiyat Fakültesi Basımevi.

Lampe, John R. and Marvin R. Jackson. 1982. *Balkan Economic History, 1550–1960.* Bloomington: Indiana University Press.

Landes, David. 1958. *Bankers and Pashas: International Finance and Economic Imperialism in Egypt.* Cambridge: Harvard University Press.

————. 1966 "Technological Change and Development in Western Europe, 1750–1914." In *The Cambridge Economic History of Europe,* Vol. VI/1, H. J. Habakkuk and M. Postan, eds., *The Industrial Revolutions and After: Incomes, Population and Technological Change,* 274–601. Cambridge: The University Press.

Leon, George. 1972. "The Greek Merchant Marine." In Stelios Papadopulos, eds., *The Greek Merchant Marine,* 13–44. Athens: National Bank of Greece.

Lewis, Arthur. 1978. *Growth and Fluctuations, 1870–1913.* London and Boston: G. Allen and Unwin.

Lewis, Bernard. 1960. "Beratlı." *Encyclopaedia of Islam,* 2nd edition, Vol. I, 1171. Leiden: E. J. Brill.

————. 1965. "The Ottoman Empire in the Mid-Nineteenth Century." *Middle Eastern Studies* I, 3 (April):283–95.

————. 1976. *The Emergence of Modern Turkey.* London: Oxford University Press.

Lilley, Samuel. 1978. "Technological Progress and the Industrial Revolution 1700-1914," Carlo M. Cipolla, eds., *The Fontana Economic History of Europe,* Vol. 3, *The Industrial Revolution.* Glasgow: Fontana/Collins.

Lybyer, A. H. 1915. "The Ottoman Turks and the Routes of Oriental Trade." *English Historical Review* XXX (October):577-88.

Mantran, Robert. 1962. *Istanbul dans la seconde Moitié du XVIIe siècle.* Paris: Librarie Adrien Maisonneuve.

Mardin, Şerif. 1962. *The Genesis of Young Ottoman Thought.* Princeton: Princeton University Press.

———. 1969. "Power, Civil Society and Culture in the Ottoman Empire." *Comparative Studies in Society and History* XI:258-81.

Marx, Karl. 1952. "The Crimean War: The Background of the Dispute (1853-1854)." In K. Marx and F. Engels, *The Russian Menace to Europe,* 120-58. Glencoe: The Free Press.

Michelsen, Edward Henry. 1853. *The Ottoman Empire and its Resources.* London: Simpkin Marshall.

Mitchell, B. R. 1981. *European Historical Statistics, 1750-1975.* New York: Facts on File.

Morawitz, Charles, 1979. *Türkiye Maliyesi.* Ankara: Maliye Bakanlığı Tetkik Kurulu Yayını. [Original: *Les Finances de la Turquie.* Paris: Guillaumin, 1902.]

Mumcu, Ahmet. 1985. *Osmanlı Devletinde Rüşvet.* İstanbul: İnkilâp Kitabevi.

Mutluçağ, Hayri. 1967. "Düyun-i Umumiye ve Reji Soygunu." *Belgelerle Türk Tarihi Dergisi* I, 2, Kasım, 33-39.

McGowan, Bruce. 1969. "Food Supply and Taxation on the Middle Danube (1508-1579)." *Archivum Ottomanicum* I:138-96.

———. 1981. *Economic Life in Ottoman Europe. Taxation Trade and the Struggle for Land, 1600-1800.* Cambridge: Cambridge University Press.

McNeill, William. 1964. *Europe's Steppe Frontier, 1500-1800.* Chicago: University of Chicago Press.

Nagata, Yuso. 1976. *Muhsinzade Mehmed Paşa ve Ayanlık Müessesesi.* Tokyo: Study of Language and Cultures of Asia and Africa, Monography Series, No. 6.

————. 1976a. *Some Documents on the Big Farms (Çiftliks) of the Notables in Western Anatolia.* Tokyo: Studia Culturae Islamicae, No. 4.

Nickoley, E. Frederick. 1924. "Agriculture." In E. G. Mears, ed., *Modern Turkey,* 280–301. New York: The Macmillan.

Ökçün, Gündüz. 1972. "19. Yüzyılın İkinci Yarısında İmalat Sanayi Alanında Verilen Ruhsat ve İmtiyazların Ana Çizgileri." *Siyasal Bilgiler Fakültesi Dergisi* XXVII:1, 136–66.

Ortaylı İlber. 1983. *İmparatorluğun En Uzun Yüzyılı.* Istanbul: Hil Yayınları.

————. 1985. *Tanzimatdan Cumhuriyete Yerel Yönetim Geleneği.* Istanbul: Hil Yayınları.

Owen, Roger. 1981. *The Middle East in the World Economy, 1800–1914.* London and New York: Methuen.

Özkaya, Yücel. 1974. "XVIII. Yźyılda Çıkarılan Adaletnamelere Göre Türkiye'nin İç Durumu." *Beleten* XXXVIII (July):445–91.

————. 1977. *Osmanlı İmparatorluğunda Ayanlık.* Ankara: A.Ü.D.T.C.F. Yayınları.

Paish, F. W. 1949. "Banking Policy and the Balance of Payments." In The American Economic Association, ed., *Readings in the Theory of International Trade,* 35–55. Philadelphia and Toronto: The Blackstone Co.

Pamuk, Şevket. 1984. *Osmanlı Ekonomisi ve Dünya Kapitalizmi (1820–1913).* Ankara: Yurt Yayıncılık.

————. 1984a. "The Ottoman Empire in the 'Great Depression' of 1873–1896." *Journal of Economic History* XLIV, 1 (March):107–118.

Paris, Robert. 1957. *Histoire du Commerce de Marseille de 1600 à 1789.* Paris: Librairie Leon.

Parvus, Efendi. 1977. *Türkiyenin Mali Tutsaklığı.* İstanbul: May Yayınları.

Paskaleva, Virginia. 1968. "Contribution aux Relations Commerciales des Provinces Balkaniques de l'Empire Ottoman Avec les États Européens au cours du XVIIIe siecle." *Etudes Historiques* IV:265–292.

Platt, D. C. M. 1971. *The Cinderella Service: British Consuls Since 1825.* London: Longman.

Polanyi, Karl. 1957. *The Great Transformation.* Boston: Beacon Press.

──────. 1971. "Economy as Instituted Process." In K. Polanyi, C. Arensberg, H. W. Pearson, eds., *Trade and Market in the Early Empires,* 243–70. Chicago: Gateway Editions.

Poroy, İbrahim İhsan. 1981. " Expansion of Opium Production in Turkey and The State Monopoly of 1828–1839." *International Journal of Middle East Studies* XIII:191–211.

Puryear, Vernon John. 1969. *Internatoinal Economics and Diplomacy in the Near East, A Study of British Commercial Policy in the Levant, 1834–1853.* Hamden: Archon Books.

Pyle, Nancy. 1977. "Ottoman Okka Weights." *Belleten* XLI:161, 115–23.

Quataert, Donald. 1973. "Ottoman Reform and Agriculture in Anatolia, 1876–1908." Unpublished Ph.D. Dissertation, University of California at Los Angeles.

──────. 1981. "Agricultural Trends and Government Policy in Ottoman Anatolia, 1800–1914." *Asian and African Studies* XV, 1 (March):69–84.

──────. 1983. *Social Disintegration and Popular Resistance in the Ottoman Empire, 1881–1908. Reactions to European Economic Penetration.* New York: New York University Press.

──────. 1986. "Machine Breaking and the Changing Carpet Industry of Western Anatolia, 1860–1908." *Journal of Social History* XIX, 3 (Spring):473–489.

Rafeq, Abdul-Karim. 1977. "Changes in the Relationship Between the Ottoman Central Administration and the Syrian Provinces from the Sixteenth to the Eighteenth Centuries." In T. Naff and R. Owen, eds., *Studies in Eighteenth Century Islamic History,* 53–73. Carbondale and Edwardsville: Southern Illinois University Press.

Research Working Group on Cyclical Rhythms and Secular Trends. 1979. "Cyclical Rhythms and Secular Trends of the Capitalist World

Economy: Some Premises, Hypotheses and Questions." *Review* II, 4 (Spring):483–500.

Robbins, Michael. 1962. *The Railway Age*. London: Routledge and Kegan Paul.

Rodkey, F. S. 1958. "Ottoman Concern About Western Economic Penetration in the Levant 1849–1856." *Journal of Modern History* XXX:348–53.

Rosenthal, Steven. 182. "Minorities and Municipal Reform in Istanbul, 1850–1870." In B. Braude and B. Lewis, eds., *Christians and Jews in the Ottoman Empire. Functioning of a Plural Society*, I, *Central Lands*, 369–85. New York and London: Holmes and Meier.

Rougon, Firmin. 1892. *Smyrne, situation commerciale et économique des pays compris dans le circonscription du consulat général de France*. Paris: Berger Levrault.

Sadat, Deena R. 1972. "Rumeli Ayanları: The Eighteenth Century." *Journal of Modern History* XLIV (Summer):346–63.

Sahillioğlu, Halil. 1968. "XVII. Yüzyıl Ortalarında Sanayi Bölgelerimiz ve Ticari İmkânları." *Belgelerle Türk Tarihi Dergisi*, I, 11, Ağustos, 61–66.

———. 1978. "Osmanlı Para Tarihinde Dünya Para ve Maden Hareketlerinin Yeri, 1300–1750." *ODTÜ Gelişme Dergisi*, Özel Sayı, 1–38.

Sakaoğlu, Necdet. 1984. *Anadolu Derebeyi Ocaklarından Köse Paşa Hanedanı*. Ankara: Yurt Yayınları.

Sarç, Ömer Celal. 1966. "Tanzimat ve Sanayimiz." In C. Issawi, ed., *The Economic History of the Middle East*, 48–59. Chicago: The University of Chicago Press.

Saul, S. B. 1969. *The Myth of Great Depression, 1873–1896*. London: The Macmillan Press.

Scherzer, Charles de (Karl ritter von). 1873. *La Province de Smyrne*. Vienne: Alfred Holder, Librarie Universitaire de Beck.

Schlote, Werner. 1951. *British Overseas Trade, From 1700 to the 1930's*. Oxford: Basil Blackwell.

Semmel, Bernard. 1970. *The Rise of Free Trade Imperialism*. Cambridge: Cambridge University Press.

Senior, Nassau William. 1859. *Journal Kept in Turkey and Greece in the Autumn of 1857 and the Beginnings of 1858.* London: Longman, Brown, Green, Logmans and Roberts.

Shaw, Stanford J. 1969. "The Origins of Representative Government in the Ottoman Empire: An Introduction to the Provincial Councils, 1839–1876." In R. B. Winder, ed. *Near Eastern Round Table, 1967–68,* 53–142. New York: New York University.

_____. 1971. *Between Old and New: The Ottoman Empire under Sultan Selim III, 1789–1807.* Cambridge: Harvard University Press.

_____. 1975. "The Nineteenth Century Ottoman Tax Reforms and Revenue System." *International Journal of Middle East Studies* VI:421–59.

Stavrianos, L. S. 1958. *The Balkans Since 1453.* New York: Rinehart and Company.

Stelle, Charles. 1940. "American Trade in Opium in China." *The Pacific Historical Review* IX, 4 (December):425–44.

Stoianovich, Traian. 1953. "Land Tenure and the Related Sectors of the Balkan Economy, 1600–1800." *Journal of Economic History* XIII, 4 (Fall):398–411.

_____. 1960. "The Conquering Balkan Orthodox Merchant." *Journal of Economic History* XX, 2 (Junc):234–313.

Sugar, P. F. and I. J. Lederer. 1969. *Nationalism in Eastern Europe.* Seattle: University of Washington Press.

Supple, Barry. 1978. "The State and the Industrial Revolution 1700–1914." In C. Cipolla, ed., *The Fontana Economic History of Europe,* Vol. III, *The Industrial Revolution,* 301–57. Glasgow: Fontana.

Sussnitzki, A. J. 1966. "Ethnic Division of Labor." In C. Issawi, ed., *The Economic History of the Middle East,* 115–25. Chicago: The University of Chicago Press.

Suvla, Rafi Şükrü. 1966. "Tanzimat Devrinde İstikrazlar" (Debts during the Tanzimat Period). In C. Issawi, ed., *The Economic History of the Middle East,* 95–106. Chicago: The University of Chicago Press.

Svoronos, N. 1956. *Le Commerce de Salonique au XVIIIe Siècle.* Paris: Presses Universitaires de France.

Temperley, Harold. 1933. "British Policy Towards Parliamentary Rule and Constitutionalism in Turkey, 1830–1914." *Cambridge Historical Journal* IV:3, 156–91.

Tengirşenk, Yusuf Kemal. 1940. "Tanzimat Devinde Osmanlı Devletinin Harici Ticaret Siyaseti." *Tanzimat* I:289–320. İstanbul: T. C. Maarif Vekaleti.

Todorov, Nikolai. 1983. *The Balkan City, 1400–1900*. Seattle and London: University of Washington Press.

Todorova, Maria. 1977. "British and Russian Policy Towards the Reform Movement in the Ottoman Empire (30's-50's of the 19th c.)." *Études Balkaniques* III:3, 17–41.

Toprak, Zafer. 1982. *Türkiyede Milli İktisat, 1980–1918*. Ankara: Yurt Yayınları.

_____. 1983. "Önemli Bir Yasa: Ölçüler Kanunu (1931)", *Yapit*, 47'2, Aralık-Ocak, 37–43.

Turan, Şerafettin. 1968. "Venedikte Türk Ticaret Merkezi." *Belleten*, XXXII, 126, Nisan, 247–283.

Turgay, Üner. 1981–1985. "The Nineteenth Century Golden Triangle: Chinese Consumption, Ottoman Production and the American Connection." *International Journal of Turkish Studies* II, 2 (Winter 1981–82):105–125; III, 1 (Winter 1984–85):65–91.

Türk Ziraat Tarihine Bir Bakış, 1938. İstanbul: Devlet Basımevi.

Ubicini, M. A. 1856. *Letters on Turkey, Part I: Turkey and the Turks*. London: John Murray. [Reprinted New York: Arno Press, 1973]

_____. 1856a. *Letters on Turkey, Part II: The Raiajs*. London: John Murray. [Reprinted New York: Arno Press, 1973]

Ülgener, Sabri. 1981. *İktisadi Cözülmenin Ahlak ve Zihniyet Dünyası*. Istanbul: Der Yayınları.

Ülker, Necmi. 1974. "The Rise of İzmir." Unpublished Ph.D. Dissertation. University of Michigan.

Uluçay, Çağatay. 1942–1944. "Karaosmanoğullarına Ait Bazı Vesikalar." *Tarih Vesikaları* II:193–207, 300–308, 434–440; III:117–126.

_____, and İbrahim Gökçen. 1939. *Manisa Tarihi*. İstanbul: Resimli Ay Matbaası.

Urquhart, David. 1833. *Turkey and its Resources.* London: Saunders and Otley, Conduit Street.

Veinstein, Gilles. 1976. "Ayan de la Région d'İzmir et Commerce du Levant (Deuxième Moitié du XVIIIe siècle)." *Études Balkaniques* XII:3, 71–83.

Velidedeoğlu, Hıfzı Veldet. 1940. "Kanunlaştırma Hareketleri ve Tanzimat." *Tanzimat* I:139–209. İstanbul: T. C. Maarif Vekaleti.

Viner, J. 1928. "International Finance and Balance of Power Diplomacy 1880–1914." *Southwestern Political and Social Science Quarterly* IX:407–51.

Wallerstein, Immanuel. 1974. *The Modern World System: Capitalist Agriculture and the Origins of the European World-Economy in the Sixteenth Century.* New York: Academic Press.

———. 1979. "The Rise and Future Demise of the World Capitalist System: Concepts for Comparative Analysis." In I. Wallerstein, *The Capitalist World-Economy,* 1–36. Cambridge: Cambridge University Press.

———. 1979a. "The Ottoman Empire and the Capitalist World-Economy: Some Questions for Research." *Review* II, 3 (Winter):389–98.

———. 1980. *The Modern World-System II: Mercantilism and the Consolidation of the European Economy 1600–1750.* New York: Academic Press.

———. 1983. *Historical Capitalism.* London: Verso.

Weber, Max. 1949. "Objective Possibility and Adequate Causation in Historical Explanation." In *The Methodology of Social Sciences,* 164–88. Glencoe: The Free Press.

Weber, Max. 1978. *Economy and Society.* Guenther Roth and Claus Wittich, eds. Berkeley: University of California Press.

Wolf, Eric. 1982. *Europe and the People Without History.* Berkeley: University of California Press.

Wood, Alfred C. 1964. *A History of the Levant Company.* New York: Barnes and Noble.

Woodruff, William. 1973. "The Emergence of an International Economy, 1700–1914." In Carlo M. Cipolla, ed., *The Fontana Economic History of Europe.* Vol. 4, *The Emergence of Industrial Societies (2),* 656–737. London and Glasgow: Collins/Fontana.

Yannoulopoulos, Yannis. 1981. "Greek Society on the Eve of Independence." In Richard Clogg, ed., *Balkan Society in the Age of Greek Independence,* 18–39. London: Macmillan.

Youngson, A. J. 1966. "The Opening Up of New Territories." In *The Cambridge Economic History of Europe,* VI, H. J. Habakkuk and M. Postan, eds., *The Industrial Revolutions and After: Incomes Population and Technological Change (1),* 139–211. Cambridge: The University Press.

Index